Profitable Preserves

HOW TO STAR [illegible] JELLY

Renee Pottle

Hestia's Hearth LLC

Hestia's Hearth LLC
PO Box 7059
Kennewick, WA 99336
Email: info@SeedtoPantry.com
SeedtoPantry.com
ReneePottle.com

ISBN: 978-0-9760137-9-2

Ordering Information: For quantity and individual purchases by corporations, associations, trade wholesalers and others, contact at the above address.

Contents

Free Customer Bonus

Go to:
PenandProvisions.com/Profitable-Preserves
or
ReneePottle.com/Profitable-Preserves

To receive:

- Printable workbook pages
- Printable copies of all checklists
- Printable copies of all image examples noted in this book
- Profitable Preserves book updates and more!

With Special Thanks To

The Ladies of the Long Table (Lynne Klippel, Kathi Laughman, Suzanne Gochenouer, Sandi Lindgren), Cindy Farler, Melinda Montgomery, Lauren Koecher, Miki Preston, Tabitha Stroup, Lisa Kivirist, and the Seed to Pantry Community. And especially to my husband, Stephen Pottle, for his decades of love and support.

Making Jam and Making Money Everything You Need to Know!

"It takes as much energy to wish as it does to plan."
Eleanor Roosevelt

Congratulations! You are about to embark on a creative journey. The kind of journey that puts cold, hard cash in your pocket. Even better - you will make this extra cash either from your own kitchen or by using a nearby facility. You will set your own hours. And you will be doing something that gives you and others pleasure. Sound too good to be true? It isn't.

Now is a particularly advantageous time to start a small jam-making business. As the years go by, we get further and further from our agrarian roots. No longer do we grow up learning how to preserve the backyard garden harvest – or even how to plant and grow a backyard garden. Life moves quickly, and between jobs, school, soccer practice, and dance lessons, there isn't much time to forage for raspberries or tend to a peach tree - let alone turn ripe fruit into jars of jewel colored jams and preserves.

As the years speed by though, we yearn for a time when things seemed simpler. A time like Grandma's good-old-days, when dinner was cooked from scratch and the pantry was filled with home preserved jams and jellies. We won't be going back to those days anytime soon, and they probably weren't as idyllic as Grandma remembered. But we can subscribe to a home food service, purchase our eggs at the local farmers' market, and buy artisan preserves made by small food producers.

Who are these talented producers? You of course! And your potential market is everywhere. According to the Specialty Foods Association, specialty jam, jelly, and other soft spread sales totaled more than $560 million in 2017. Currently (2020), specialty food sales are growing at a rate triple that of other retail categories. Mordor Intelligence, a marketing intelligence firm, expects that the jam, jelly, and preserves market will continue to grow over the next five years, especially in the organic/natural/clean label – artisan - arena.

Artisan - what we used to call homemade - soft spreads are an affordable luxury, providing authentic flavor and evoking a simpler time. Customers are seeking a product bursting with fruit flavor, reminiscent of Grandma's kitchen.

Homemade jams and other soft spreads are good product options for the prospective entrepreneur. Authentic luxuries like artisan jam or unique preserves are always in demand. And because your home-crafted soft spreads are affordable, your business will be less affected by economic ups and downs. When the nation's economic situation is on a downward slide, we stock our shelves with kitchen staples. When the economy is booming, we indulge in fine restaurant dining. But whether boom or bust, we happily purchase jars of beautiful, jewel-toned, artisan jelly, because they are an affordable delight.

You have the power to successfully meet this need. Don't worry – this guide will be your trusty companion every step of the way. It's easy, I promise!

This book shows you how to start a one or two-person jam, jelly, or other soft spread business. It takes you step-by step-through the process, turning a seemingly overwhelming journey into an enjoyable jaunt, and a profitable venture.

> *It is more common than you might think; getting carried away with a hobby. Before you know it, stuffed animals fill every corner, model railroads take over the garage, or jars of soft spreads fill entire cupboards. Instead of investing in extra shelf space, turn your hobby into a money maker. For example, I started writing cookbooks to justify my huge cookbook collection. Now when I purchase a new cookbook, it's considered research!*

Read the guide from beginning to end, then turn back to each section as you set up your business and start selling jams, jellies, and more!

Let's begin with a few assumptions:

- **You are a homemade jam enthusiast**. You have some experience making jam, jelly, fruit butter, or other soft spreads from scratch. You know, or are willing to learn, how to safely process these products too.

- **You want to make extra money**. This guide will help you turn your jam-making hobby into a small or micro-business. Want to earn extra money for the holidays or for travel or to put in a swimming pool? Start here.

- **You want to start small**. Your jam making business will be a part-time, small, or seasonal endeavor, providing extra income. It may grow into your primary source of income in the future, but for now you are starting small. By starting small, you will either operate as a one-person solopreneur or in conjunction with a partner or occasional helper.

- **You will self-fund (low) start-up costs**. This book will show you how to start your jam business on a tiny budget, sometimes less than $1000. The goal is to self-fund your start-up, or borrow funds from family/friends. Self-funding means you won't spend valuable time investing in a massive business plan with five-year financial projections. Banks require that kind of input before lending, but you'll be spending that time working on your business instead, getting closer to actual *cash in hand* instead of designing presentations for bankers or venture capitalists.

- **You have a defined motivation**. Maybe you have a few backyard fruit-trees that produce too much fruit for your family, and you would like to monetize the over-supply. Or maybe you are looking for a way to earn some money from home. Perhaps you get carried away every summer making jars and jars of jam, and your family couldn't possibly eat it all.

Making jam or jelly may come easily to you. But you probably have all kinds of questions about starting a food-related business, safety requirements, licenses, equipment, and more. Don't worry. We will walk through it together with this step-by-step guide. Soon you will be making jam ***and*** making money. Let's get started!

Let's define your beginning business ideas. Write the answers on the next page so you won't forget!

Will your business be a one-person endeavor? Or a two or three-person endeavor? Or some other configuration?

Will it be seasonal? If so, which season? Spring? Summer? Fall? Winter? Holiday?

Or will it be a year-round part-time gig?

Do you have a specific goal in mind? I.E., making enough money for a vacation or to supplement your family income?

Where will you obtain your start-up funds?

Notes

CHAPTER 1

Profitable Products Choosing Soft Spreads to Make and Sell

> *"What I wanted was to be allowed to do the thing in the world that I did best – which I believed then and believe now is the greatest privilege there is. When I did that, success found me."*
> *Debbi Fields*

Before we even think about business licenses, legal requirements, and what you will name your business, let's make some tasty decisions. Don't panic! These aren't Sophie's Choice-type decisions. They can be changed or tweaked later if you change your mind.

Selecting Your Favorite Soft Spreads

We use the term, *soft spreads*, to collectively describe jam, jelly, fruit butter, conserves, preserves, and marmalade.

The first step is to identify the soft spreads that you already *know how* to prepare, and those that you *enjoy* making. It's a good idea to start your business offering products that you enjoy creating. For example, while I *know how* to make jelly, and make a few jars every year, I don't necessarily *love* making jelly.

On the other hand, I do like making fruit butters. I enjoy experimenting with creative fruit combinations, and I like the more relaxed cooking method. You may feel the exact opposite; maybe you enjoy how fast jelly sets up and detest the messy fruit butter puréeing process. If you are making several batches of the same soft spread week after week, it should be a soft spread you enjoy preserving.

Close your eyes and envision yourself at the stove, stirring a bubbling pot of your favorite soft spreads. What are you making? Are the jars filled with crimson red raspberry jam? Royal purple jelly? Sunny apricot butter? Take a few minutes and capture your thoughts in the notes section at the end of this chapter. Which of your favorite soft spreads came readily to mind? What products did you see yourself making?

Types of Soft Spreads

Soft spreads, like chocolates, come in many textures and varieties. While a box of chocolates might have nuts and jellies, crèmes and caramels, in the soft spread world we have jams and preserves, marmalades and fruit butters. Often, we call them all *jam*. But what makes a jam? Or a conserve? Or a fruit butter? The differences are subtle but the results can be vastly different. You wouldn't ask someone if they wanted a chocolate crème and then hand them a caramel, so let's keep our soft spreads separate too!

Jams

Jams are a combination of slightly crushed or thinly sliced fruit and sugar, cooked until a soft gel. There may be other ingredients added, lemon juice for example, but basically jam is just crushed fruit and sugar. All fruits can be used to make jam, but berries work especially well.

Jelly

Like all soft spreads, jelly is a combination of fruit, acid, and sugar. Jellies however, are made from fruit juice and have no included fruit pieces. Jelly sets up firmer than any other soft spread. Many people use commercial pectin to assure a firm jelly set. Apples, tart cherries, grapes and other high pectin fruits are especially suited to making jelly.

Fruit Butters

Fruit butters are the easiest soft spreads to make. They are simply puréed fruit and sugar cooked together until thick. Fruit butters use less sugar than most soft spreads. They can be enhanced with lemon juice, herbs, alcohol spirits, or other ingredients. Fruits that caramelize well with long cooking, like apples and peaches, make luscious fruit butters.

Preserves

Preserves are similar to jam and the two are often confused. Here's the difference; jam is made from crushed fruit while preserves are made from chopped fruit. The chopped fruit is macerated, or steeped, in sugar so that the pieces hold their shape during the cooking process. Peaches, cherries and other firm fruits make excellent preserves.

Marmalades

Marmalades can be made from almost any fruit, but must include thinly sliced citrus peel. Traditional marmalades are made only from citrus, and are more bitter than other soft spreads. Other marmalades might include cherries or berries along with the oranges, lemons and/or limes.

Conserves

Similar in texture to jams or preserves, conserves usually include dried fruits like raisins or coconut along with fresh fruits. Nuts are often added too. Because of this, conserves are less likely to be served spread on your toast, and more likely to adorn a pork chop or cheese plate.

Fruit Curds

Fruit curds like lemon curd or orange curd are also considered soft spreads. Fruit curds are a combination of eggs, butter, citrus juice, and sugar that are slowly cooked until thickened. While fruit curds are delicious, because they contain eggs they cannot be made at home if you plan to sell them to the public. Due to their lower acid level, preparing fruit curds at a commercial kitchen may also require additional licenses.

Choosing Your Product Offerings

It's easy to excitedly over-commit when starting a jam business. Maybe you make 32 different kinds of jam for your family each year. Each type is fun to create and tastes delicious. Obviously, your future customers would love each and every variety!

But keeping track of the numerous ingredients needed for such a large offering will be time consuming, especially if you are starting this business by yourself. Before you know it, your facility will be full of fresh fruit and labels, and you have run out of time to prepare any jam.

Ingredients needed for creating 10 cases of peach jam will cost less than ingredients needed for creating two cases each of peach, plum, cherry, pear, and apricot jam. The cost of each individual fruit usually decreases per pound when buying in bulk. For example, one pound of peaches may cost $1.99 per pound, but 20 pounds purchased at once may only cost $20.

It's best to start with fewer product selections, until you have established a market for your products and perfected the cooking process. In addition, depending upon your State, each recipe may need a licensing agency approval. Paying to have two or three recipes approved is less expensive than paying to have 32 different recipes approved!

On the other hand, maybe you make a killer peach butter and nothing else. Is just one type of soft spread enough for a viable business? It might be, but making soft spreads as a business is different from making soft spreads for your family. You should provide enough variety to keep your customers interested, but not so many different products that you exhaust yourself, or your budget, trying to keep all varieties in stock.

A good rule of thumb is to start your business by offering three different products.

- It could be three different jams; like strawberry jam, peach jam, and tomato jam.
- Or it could be three different spreads with one theme like; apricot jam, apricot syrup, and apricot conserve.

Is Your Recipe Legal?

Before you make a final decision about your jam products, you must ask yourself, "Is it possible to legally prepare my desired recipe?"

You are starting a jam business to add cash to your pocket. Finding yourself in legal trouble will deplete that cash quickly. It's best to avoid legal issues – even of the *jammy* kind.

Many states limit which recipes can be prepared in your home. If you decide to run a cottage industry from home (find more information about cottage industry businesses in Chapter 2), you may have to adjust your desired recipe.

For example, you will probably not be allowed to make your famous Cabernet Jelly from the bottles of wine you stockpiled over the last decade. Your whole family may love this jelly. It might be just the thing customers in your town are seeking. But state laws regarding the manufacture and selling of alcohol products are strict, and home production is not allowed.

On the other hand, if you want to make jelly from Cabernet grapes – before they are turned into wine, it is considered no different than Concord Grape Jelly. Grapes are grapes.

Another potential stumbling block is making soft spreads using low-acid fruits and vegetables like banana jam or pepper jelly. It may still be possible to prepare these products from your cottage industry home kitchen, depending on your home state. However, be aware that most states only allow low-acid spreads to be made in a certified kitchen using an approved recipe.

We will further explore this topic in Chapter 2, but for now keep the above product limitations in mind.

What is Your USP? (Unique Selling Point)

Every business has a defined USP for its products. The unique selling point helps differentiate your product in the marketplace. Your USP doesn't have to be mind-blowing or culture-changing. But it should be easily defined. Some common food product USPs are:

Price: Some companies offer the *lowest price*, marketing to budget-minded families. Other companies sell their products for highly inflated prices, offering luxury and exclusivity.

Fresh: This USP is often used for products that have a short shelf-life and need to be refrigerated. It can also be used for products like jams that are made from fresh, farm-grown fruits.

All-Natural: The government is currently trying to define just what *all-natural* means, but for most small food manufacturers and consumers, the term *all-natural* means products made without chemical additives or preservatives.

Unique Flavors: Your local grocery store sells blackberry jam and orange marmalade. But you probably won't find blackberry-maple jam or Meyer lemon marmalade. Unique and unusual flavors might be the best USP for you.

Eat Local: *Eat local* is a popular USP for small food businesses, especially if you live in a thriving tourist area. For example, I purchase cactus jelly whenever I am in Arizona, and lilikoi curd in Hawaii. Is your area known for a specialty fruit, herb, or other flavor?

Simply Homemade: The world is starting to notice that we have lost touch with our food, that most of it is full of ingredients we don't recognize and can't pronounce. People yearn for a simpler time, a time when homemade meant *made with love*. Sometimes that's all we need as a USP – simple and homemade, with love.

Nostalgia: This USP is similar, but slightly different from Simply Homemade. Nostalgia works especially well if you plan to bring back some old-time favorites that have disappeared over the years. Do you make your great-grandmother's chokecherry jelly? Maybe nostalgia is the USP for you.

Organic: Organic products are more popular every year. There seems to be no end to the number of food items that are labeled organic. This is a good USP for specialty soft spreads, however there are quite a few competitors. The term *organic* is strictly defined by the U.S. Government. If you label your products *organic*, or *made with organic ingredients*, the ingredients must meet the approved definition.

According to the U. S. Department of Agriculture (USDA), organic foods are not treated with synthetic pesticides or fertilizers, and are not genetically modified organisms (GMOs).

Artisan: The artisan USP is related to *Simply Homemade*, but with a more illustrious pedigree. Artisans are expert craftsmen, producing unique, high-quality goods. While *Simply Homemade* evokes Nana's farm fresh products, *Artisan* calls to mind the village sweet shop, where aproned experts stirred their jam creations in the big copper pot behind the wood and glass counter.

The most successful USPs for a specialty food like homemade jams and jellies are usually: Nostalgia, Simply Homemade, Eat Local, Unique Flavors, and Artisan. All-natural and Fresh can also be used, although there are some indications that consumers no longer trust the *all-natural* label.

I do not recommend that you use Price as a USP. A specialty product, made by hand from fresh ingredients, will never be able to compete with commercially prepared soft spreads found on every grocery store shelf. These companies have large factories and large budgets. Your product is unique, don't try to compete with Smuckers® or store brands.

On the other hand, while you are preparing a specialty jam, that by its very nature will be more expensive than a ubiquitous brand, you cannot charge more than the market will bear. Consumers may happily spend $8 for a jar of your homemade apple butter, but they will not spend $80 for that same jar. Companies whose USP is *high price* offer prestige and exclusivity; companies like Tiffany or Rolex®. Few food products fall into this category.

Do you find yourself drawn to one or two of these USPs? Write down those you find especially appealing. Again, don't worry – it can be changed later. The important thing is that you now are well on your way to a viable business!

Do You Need an Academic Degree or Certificate?

If you practice law, you need a professional degree and to pass the bar exam. If you set up a salon, you need a hairdresser certificate. But anyone can make and sell jam. However, enrolling in a class or certificate program is a good way to increase your jam making confidence and abilities. It's always a good idea to be up-to-date. If you are still making jam the same way you did 25 years ago, maybe it's time to modernize the process.

Luckily you don't have to invest years in a college degree. There are several programs available; some near your home and others you can access online.

Master Food Preserver

This is the Cadillac of training programs. The Master Food Preserver program is sponsored by land grant universities. The program covers much more than just how to make jam. It also covers food safety issues, safe home canning methods for both high-acid and low-acid foods, and how to prevent foodborne illness.

Usually lasting about 40 hours, the program often has a volunteer component, expanding the reach of each trained advisor. The program varies slightly in each state, meeting specific local needs.

Call your local Cooperative Extension office to see if there is a program near you. Although land grant universities are found in every U. S. state, not every state hosts a Master Food Preserver program. Let your local Cooperative Extension office know that you are interested in attending a Master Food Preserver program, and they may start a program in your area.

Online Trainings

Most short, online training programs can be completed in a few hours. The National Center for Home Food

Preservation has an online program you can access through their website: https://nchfp.uga.edu/. In addition, some local universities have put parts of their Master Food Preserver Programs online. Contact your local Cooperative Extension Agency to see if your state is offering an online program this year.

Local Trainings

You may be able to find a home food preservation training class locally, either through your community education program or through local businesses. If so, make sure that the instructors are familiar with up-to-date materials and safety knowledge.

Let's review your business ideas:

Which three products will you start with? Don't worry, you can always change your mind by the time you finish this guide. The important thing is to get started with some products in mind.

What is your USP? Again, don't worry – it can be changed later. The important thing is that you now are well on your way to a viable business!

Should you update your food preservation skills? What kind of training works best for you? How and when will you access the training?

Notes

CHAPTER 2

The Home or Away Challenge Finding the Space to Make Your Products

> *"When in doubt, bootstrap. Using your own personal resources is the easiest way to start a business. You don't have to convince investors about the merits of your idea. You just have to convince yourself."* Ryan Holmes, *co-founder of Hootsuite*

Your business is off to a great start. You have identified three initial products to make and sell, you've chosen an USP, and you have updated your skills. Now it's time to figure out, "Where will I make my luscious jams and other soft spreads?"

Since you are starting small, there are usually two cost-effective options to consider. You could make your products at home following cottage industry regulations. Or you could use certified kitchen space as a small food manufacturer/processor.

Cottage Industry

Operating a cottage industry means that you can make products to sell, right in your own kitchen. Cottage industry businesses are legal in most states now, but there are restrictions. While most low-risk foods like jams, jellies, and other soft spreads can be made in your home kitchen, riskier soft spreads like banana jam or lemon curd usually cannot be made under cottage industry regulations.

This business type's primary advantage is that is that you can prepare your jam and other soft spread products in the comfort of your own kitchen, whenever you want, day or night. You won't be paying additional overhead charges like rent or transportation, and often you can use the cooking equipment that has already found a home in your kitchen.

A cottage industry's primary disadvantage is that local and state guideline limits may stifle your business creativity. Some states severely regulate which fruits can be used to make jams or jellies in a home kitchen. You may be able to make peach jam at home, but the state may not allow persimmon jam. You may not be able to make conserves or marmalades at all in your home kitchen, only jams, jellies, and fruit butters. You probably won't be able to make any product that includes eggs – like lemon or orange curd.

Some states require a separate storage area and that separate equipment be used, instead of your personal kitchen equipment. Therefore, you will lose some of your storage space to redundant equipment. You will most likely need a written plan that identifies how you will keep young children and pets out of the kitchen when you are working. Despite these limitations, cottage industry may be exactly the business model you are seeking. It certainly is less expensive than other models.

All states that allow cottage industry businesses limit where and how you can sell your products. Many states allow only in-person sales, meaning that you will most likely sell your products at farmers' markets or artisan fairs. Some states let you ship product – thus opening the door to selling via your own website or Etsy, but most states do not allow this practice. Wholesale and consignment sales are usually not allowed.

As each state is different, it's best to review the requirements at your location before deciding whether a cottage industry is right for you. Here in Washington state for example, cottage food proprietors can't legally sell more than $25,000 of product each year. We can make bakery goods, granola, most candies, and jams, jellies, and preserves at home, but pickles, juices, BBQ sauces, and dog treats aren't allowed. Several licenses are required to operate a cottage industry business, including a master business license, a food handler's card, a cottage food permit, and health department approval.

My native state of Maine lets cottage food businesses make and sell baked goods, pickles, salsa, and jams/jellies. For most products, you only need a home food processors license and a quality home inspection. Arizona's cottage food law lets you make many different kinds of breads and even chocolate covered strawberries at home, but you can't make jams, jellies, and other soft spreads. On the other hand, the only license you need is a health department registration and a food handler's card. Rhode Island only allows farmers who are selling value-added products to create products in their home kitchens, and New Jersey doesn't allow cottage industry products at all.

It was a busy day – but then, most days were busy. Each morning started the usual way, dragging the kids out of bed, helping them get ready for school, and then walking the 15 minutes up the hill to reach the elementary school. Once back at home, I settled into my office routine, catching up on my two solo-businesses. It was always a rush, trying to get professional phone calls completed and planning tasks organized before the Kindergartener returned home at noon.

When the phone rang, I assumed it was probably the client I was expecting that morning. Instead, it was a neighbor. We walked our children to school together, so she had a good idea of my schedule. No, it wasn't an emergency, at least not for me. But it was pretty important to her. "Hey," Jill said, "Carrie just got hired at the Inn." "Great," I responded, wondering why this news couldn't wait until our next trek up the hill. "Well," she continued, "we thought maybe you would babysit for her since you don't work or anything."

For some reason, when we work from home, others think that we don't work. For many, this will be the biggest business struggle. Sadly, it won't just be clueless neighbors who feel this way. Friends and family may also intrude on your business time when they need a ride to the store, they have a sick child, or the dress they are wearing to this weekend's event needs to be picked up from the dry cleaners NOW!

Your jam and jelly business may be a side-gig. You may only make and sell soft spreads during the holidays. It may be a tiny business, where you only plan to sell enough product to pay your monthly gym membership. Either way, it is still your business, and deserves to be treated as such. Your hours need to work for YOU.

As a serial side-gig entrepreneur, I have operated several tiny home businesses over the past 30 years. I did clothing alterations for a wedding shop while my infant dozed in our two-room apartment. I made custom children's clothing and draperies while the boys were in pre-school. I sold numerous items at craft fairs while my tweens and their father biked, hiked, and treated each new area like an adventure. And I made specialty foods at a commercial kitchen while the number of grandchildren continued to grow.

After years of squeezing hours to find a few minutes here and there, my advice is; set a weekly schedule with at least a few hours devoted to your business. During this scheduled time, you may be preparing your products, working on marketing materials, or paying the bills. Doing so helps you treat the business like a professional. When those intruding on your time respond with, "You can flex your schedule," answer honestly, "No, I can't," and don't feel guilty. If you had a part-time job at the local grocery store would these same people ask you to rearrange your work schedule? Most likely not.

Despite all of this, many of us create our part-time business so that we can still help friends and family when needed. So, some interruptions may be ok with you. For example, I am happy to pick a sick child up from school, even if it's during my scheduled working hours. But dry cleaning and grocery store runs do not change my schedule. Remember the old coffee cup saying, *Failure to plan on your part does not constitute an emergency on my part*? It's a good motto to live by, especially when trying to run a business from home.

Small Food Manufacturer/Processor

Maybe a cottage industry enterprise isn't for you. Perhaps you want to sell products wholesale or make a soft spread using less-common ingredients. In that case, operating as a small food manufacturer/processor and producing your products in a commercial/certified kitchen is the best option. Don't fret. Finding commercial kitchen space may not be as onerous as you fear. Many churches and social groups have commercial kitchen space available and are happy to rent it during their off hours.

You may also be able to rent space at a nearby food incubator. Food incubators are popping up all over the country. Some are operated as non-profit businesses, some are for-profit businesses, and some are operated by municipal or regional government. A food incubator is basically a commercial/certified kitchen that meets state and/or federal guidelines. You, as the food manufacturer rent space there to prepare your product.

For example, when my husband and I operated our specialty food business, we rented space at a municipal food incubator. We only rented the actual hours needed to prepare our current orders, and build up our inventory. At this particular incubator, we requested needed hours and days, based on a first-come, first-serve basis. The incubator was open 24 hours a day, 7 days a week. We had no minimum monthly hour requirement, but many incubators do require a 20-hour monthly commitment.

Commercial/certified kitchens can be found all around you. Any food preparation space that is approved by the local health authority is considered a commercial/certified kitchen. If there is no food incubator in your area, seek out other certified kitchen space like Grange Hall kitchens, Elks' Lodges, private school kitchens and bakery or restaurant space. Tabitha Stroup and her partner of *Friend in Cheeses Jam Company,* started their business using meeting-hall kitchens. "We looked for inexpensive space that no one else was using," she says. As the business grew, eventually they were able to build their own commercial kitchen.

Renting commercial kitchen space gives you more product flexibility. For example, you may not be legally able to make your famous ginger conserve from home, but once the recipe is approved by a food testing lab, it can be made in a commercial kitchen. Unlike cottage industry businesses, products prepared in a commercial kitchen can be sold online, through sales representatives, wholesale or retail. Renting space in a commercial kitchen may save you money, since the kitchen already has commercial-grade equipment like a sanitizing dishwasher, large food processors, and ample refrigerator space. A commercial kitchen also offers much more counter space than even the most luxurious home kitchen, letting you keep all your ingredients within reach.

Operating as a small food manufacturer/processor means getting a state Department of Agriculture food processor license instead of a cottage industry license. See more about necessary licenses in Chapter 5.

Build Your Own Commercial Kitchen

There is a third option–building your own certified/commercial kitchen. Building your own commercial kitchen may seem like a crazy idea at first, but if you have an unused garage, outbuilding, or basement space, setting up a commercial kitchen could solve your business problem. As you might expect there are laws that will guide you along this path.

Start by contacting the local health department. They will provide the most-up to-date local requirements and acceptable floor plans for your own kitchen. The best time to do this is before you start any remodel job. Every state or municipality will, of course, have their own rules; rules that may seem strange, weird, or downright anti-business. It's best to be aware of them before you start remodeling. The health department will know who you need to talk to and how to move forward quickly. They may even know which local facility is closing and has equipment for sale!

A commercial kitchen requires specialized equipment; for example, a 3-bin sink, a sanitizing dishwasher, or specialized jam making equipment. You can often find this equipment via Craigslist postings or when a local restaurant is going out of business.

Are you handy? Then remaking your garage into a commercial kitchen may be just the job for you! Do keep in mind that building your kitchen will be a construction job, meaning local or regional electrical and plumbing inspectors must approve your project, in addition to state or local certifications. Remember to get your municipal building permits too.

Your State Department of Agriculture will need to sign off on your new kitchen before you can start using it to make and sell soft spreads. They will consider your water source, sanitation plan, and how you plan to dispose of your garbage.

Building your own commercial kitchen provides the best of both worlds; you can make any approved recipe while still working at or near home. Your space is your own, you do not have to request kitchen time in advance, you do not have to drag equipment from home to rental facility, and you may even be able to rent out your kitchen a few hours a week to some other aspiring food entrepreneur, thus turning your kitchen into a money maker.

Although this is a fantastic option that seems to solve all problems, there are a few disadvantages. Building a commercial kitchen may require space you do not have. I always coveted my own commercial kitchen, but there just wasn't room in my home or on my in-town house lot. Or your local municipal code may not allow a manufacturing facility in your backyard, no matter how small or attractive the building.

There is no denying that building your own facility requires a large up-front expense. Most people see this option as something they will build later, once their business is up and running.

Now it's time to review. Consider:

Will you operate your business from home as a cottage food industry? Or will you pursue a small food manufacturer/processor approach? Or what about building your own commercial kitchen? Is that a viable option for you?

If as a cottage food industry: how will you keep pets out of the kitchen? How will you sanitize your processing area? Do you have enough storage space for your supplies and ingredients?

If as a small food manufacturer/processor: Where will you find certified kitchen space that you can afford? Is it possible to also store your ingredients and equipment there? Or will you have to bring these items each time you prepare products?

Do you have the space and expertise to build your own commercial kitchen? Where will you put it? Where will you get the necessary equipment? Who will build it for you? How long will it be before it is completed?

Notes

CHAPTER 3

The Science of Soft Spreads Ensuring a Successful Batch of Jam

> *"Begin always expecting good things to happen."* Tom Hopkins

You don't have to be a chemist or microbiologist to successfully make and sell delicious soft spreads. No lab coats or test tubes are needed to turn out beautiful jars of jelly. But, cooking, canning, and preserving all result in scientific reactions – even if we don't think of the processes from a scientific point of view. Therefore, a basic understanding of the parts of jam helps ensure that each batch turns out perfectly.

What is Pectin?

If you paid attention in nutrition class, you may remember that there are two types of fiber; soluble and insoluble.

Insoluble fiber provides roughage. It's the type of fiber that doesn't break down much in our digestive tract, but acts like a road sweeper keeping everything moving along. Wheat or oat bran, beans and nuts are all good sources of insoluble fiber.

Soluble fiber dissolves in water to form a gel. Soluble fiber helps us feel full longer, and helps to lower cholesterol and blood sugar. Sweet potatoes, Brussels sprouts, and avocados are all good sources of soluble fiber.

Pectin is a type of soluble fiber found in most plants, especially fruits. Pectin is what helps a pot of cooking fruit and sugar form a thickened gel, or jam.

Which Fruits are Naturally High in Pectin?

Although all fruits contain some natural pectin, certain fruits have higher levels than others:

- Crab apples and other sour apples
- Sour, under-ripe blackberries
- Concord grapes
- Cranberries
- Quince
- Lemons and limes

- Most plums
- Bitter oranges

Which Fruits are Naturally Low in Pectin?

- Blueberries
- Pears
- Raspberries
- Strawberries
- Sweet cherries

Which Fruits Fall in the Middle?

All over-ripe fruits contain less pectin than their under-ripe counterparts. Thus, ripe blackberries have less pectin than sour, under-ripe blackberries.

Also, certain varieties of the same fruit will have more pectin than other varieties. For example, bitter Seville oranges are high pectin, but sweet oranges are less so. I have always found mangoes to have a large amount of pectin (as do some agricultural experts), but others find mangoes to be low in pectin. No doubt the amount of pectin in the mango on your kitchen counter depends on where that mango was grown, and whether or not it is ripe. In general, the following fruits have a medium level of pectin:

- Sweet apples
- Most grapes
- Oranges
- Papayas
- Peaches

- Apricots
- Kiwis
- Grapefruit
- Tangerines
- Rhubarb

How to Add Pectin to Jam

Since we make jam from all of the above fruits, even those with low pectin levels, there must be a way to increase the pectin level – otherwise the jam would never gel! A few ways to do this are:

Traditional long-cooking jams: The fruit mixture is cooked for a long period, leading to a thickened, slightly caramelized jam. See more about long-cooking jams later in this chapter.

Liquid pectin: We can purchase liquid pectin to add to the hot fruit mixture, allowing the jam to gel. This is a quicker method than traditional jams. Liquid pectin will only work correctly when following a recipe specifically written for liquid pectin.

Powdered Pectin: We can also purchase powdered pectin. Powdered pectin is usually mixed with fruit before heating, and then sugar is added after the pectin powder is dissolved.

Both commercially prepared liquid pectin and powdered pectin are made from apple or citrus peel. Both result in a sturdier, more formed gel than most traditional jams.

Low-sugar pectin: There are several types of commercial low-sugar pectin that can be used to make jam. They are still a pectin product, but have been modified to work a bit differently.

Homemade pectin: Back in the old days, before commercially prepared pectin was available, creative cooks made their own pectin to assure jam gel. Although it now seems like unnecessary work, you may want to make your own pectin too.

How to Make Homemade Pectin

I almost never use commercial pectin when making jam. I prefer a softer gel set than commercial pectin provides, and I prefer the flavor of long-cooking jams. Plus, commercial pectin causes some people to experience stomach distress. So, if you find that purchased jam gives you a belly ache, it's probably the added pectin.

Also, you may want to avoid commercial pectin for other reasons. Commercial pectin includes preservatives, and is most often made from GMO corn sugar (dextrose). Thus, if your USP (Unique Selling Point) is *All-Natural or Organic*, be sure you are using an appropriate pectin product.

While you can make *jam* without adding pectin using the long-cooking method, *jelly* must be made either with naturally high-pectin fruit like crabapples, or with added pectin. Luckily, it's easy to make your own pectin that can then be used to make jelly or to decrease jam setting time.

1. Put 8 cups of apple cores, peels, or chopped apples into a large pot. Tart apples work best.
2. Add a couple of cups of water, enough to cover the bottom of the pan plus some extra, but not so much that it covers all of the apples.
3. Bring to a boil, reduce heat and simmer until everything is soft and mushy.
4. Strain, using a jelly bag.
5. The remaining juice is liquid pectin. To make jelly, use equal parts homemade pectin and fruit juice.

You can store homemade pectin in the refrigerator for up to five days, or freeze it to use later.

The Role of Sugar

Making jam is a fairly simple project, but there are a few basic requirements. Just like you can't (usually) make a big loaf of bread without flour, water, and yeast; you can't (usually) make jam without pectin, sugar, and acid.

How Much Sugar Do I Need to Make Jam?

In general, long-cooking jams require less sugar than quick-cooking jams.

- A long-cooking jam is a combination of fruit, sugar, and acid, cooked until the mixture gels.
- A quick-cooking jam brings fruit and sugar to a boil, then adds commercially prepared *liquid* pectin to form a gel.

- Or, a quick-cooking jam combines fruit and *powdered* pectin, brings them to a boil, and then adds sugar.

Long-cooking jams use about 4 parts of fruit to 3 parts of sugar. So, a recipe that calls for 4 cups of berries needs 3 cups of sugar to properly gel.

Quick-cooking jams require nearly an equal amount of sugar as fruit, and sometimes even more sugar than fruit. A recipe that calls for 4 cups of berries needs anywhere between 3 ½ – 5 cups of sugar for the jam to gel.

Fruit butters, which are thickened by cooking and puréeing fruit and sugar until the desired texture, require half as much sugar as fruit. A recipe that calls for 4 cups of fruit purée needs only 2 cups of sugar. The difference is because fruit butters don't gel, they cook down into a more concentrated form.

Honey, Brown Sugar, and Maple Syrup

Honey or pure maple syrup can be substituted for some of the sugar when making jam. This is especially true when making a long-cooking jam. You can replace half of the sugar with either honey or maple syrup. I often use honey with peach or pear jams, and maple syrup is lovely with blackberries or cranberries. Be sure to use 100% pure maple syrup, not maple flavored pancake syrups, for rich maple flavor. Keep in mind that if you are operating a cottage industry enterprise from home, your state may not allow honey to be used in soft spreads.

Brown sugar can be used instead of granulated white sugar. Brown sugar lends a caramelized flavor and a darker color to soft spreads. Remember that sugar made from sugar beets is almost certainly GMO, and cannot be used when your USP is *Organic*, and shouldn't be used if your USP is *All-Natural*. Cane sugar, while more expensive, should be used in these situations.

Low-Sugar Soft Spreads

Over and over I am asked, "Can I use less sugar when making jam?". We all want more jam – but less sugar! I understand, but we cannot haphazardly reduce the sugar content in our jam recipe. Only recipes that have been specifically developed for a commercially prepared low-sugar pectin can be made with less sugar. Why, you ask?

Why is Sugar Important for Soft Spreads?

Sugar isn't just sweet on the tongue, it's a hard worker too, doing several necessary jobs in every batch of jam.

Fruit Stability: Have you ever made preserves? Preserves are made by macerating, or steeping, chopped pieces of fruit in sugar, and then cooking the combination until it gels. Instead of the fruit cooking down into a *jammy* concoction, the end result is almost like fruit pieces suspended in jelly. The sugar helps the chopped fruit retain its shape and texture.

Gel: Sugar is one of the three necessary components for jam set, or gel. Sugar molecules grab onto water molecules as the mixture is heated. This allows the pectin to form a gel. If there is too little sugar added, the pectin will be diluted and will not form a gel.

Keeps Bacteria Away: Sugar molecules can be quite thirsty and like to pull as much water away from the mixture as they can. As a result, they also pull water from any microbes that are lurking around. Just like we can't live without water, neither can microbes. When sugar pulls the water out of the microbe cells, it effectively kills them. This makes sugar an excellent food preserver, if enough is added to the mixture.

What About Low-Sugar Jams?

As mentioned above, low-sugar jams can be made only using low-sugar pectin products like Ball® RealFruit® Low or No-Sugar Needed Pectin or Pomona's Universal Pectin™. You must also use a recipe designed for a low-sugar pectin for the jam to successfully set.

Low-sugar jams have a shorter shelf life than long-cooking or quick-cooking jams.

Some freezer jams also use less sugar, because they only need enough sugar to form a gel, not enough to actually preserve the product since it is stored in the freezer. However, other freezer jam recipes use large amounts of sugar – so read your recipe carefully.

Whew! That was a lot of explaining to answer a simple question. Basically, it boils down to:

- No, you can't use less sugar in your jam recipe, and

- Be sure to follow the recipe you have chosen!

High-Acid vs Low-Acid

Making jam successfully requires 3 basic components; pectin, sugar, and acid. Much like sugar, acid has a couple of different roles in jam making.

Brightness and Flavor: Have you ever added a splash of vinegar to French fries or a bowl of tasteless soup? Squeezed lemon over poached fish? Piled chopped, fresh tomatoes on a plate of pasta? If so, you have enhanced the flavor of a mild food (potatoes, white fish, pasta) by adding a bit of acid. Adding acid to jam works the same way. Adding a little lemon juice increases the fruit flavor of your jam.

Gel: Peter Yarrow, Noel Paul Stookey, and Mary Travers were (are) all fantastic singers separately. But when they formed a trio, Peter, Paul, and Mary created magic. We get the same – albeit less musical – harmony when we combine pectin, sugar, and acid. All three are needed to form a perfect jam gel. Sugar slurps up the water, while acid acts as a matchmaker between pectin molecules, allowing the jam to set up correctly. Some fruits have enough natural acid so they don't need any added to the mixture. Other fruits always need added acid.

Which Fruits are Naturally High in Acid?

In addition to the following high-acid fruits, all under-ripe fruits have more acid than their ripe or over-ripe counterparts:

- Cranberries
- Most citrus fruits
- Quince
- Rhubarb
- Pineapple
- Kiwi

Which Fruits are Naturally Low in Acid?

In addition to the following low-acid fruits, all over-ripe fruits are lower in acid than their under-ripe or ripe counterparts:

- Sweet cherries
- Apricots
- Peaches
- Pears
- Figs
- Plums
- Nectarines

Which Fruits Fall in the Middle?

The following fruits fall in between the high/low extremes:

- Apples

- Most berries
- Mangoes
- Guavas
- Sweet oranges

How to Add Acid to Jam

When making jam, use a combination of some under-ripe fruit along with ripe and over-ripe fruit.

If you are making jam from a low-acid fruit, like peaches, be sure to add lemon juice or citric acid. Usually we add about 1 Tablespoon of lemon juice to each pound of fruit used in the batch. You can also use 1/8 teaspoon of powdered citric acid if you prefer – citric acid can usually be found at the health food store. Be aware however, that commercially prepared citric acid powder is considered a food additive. Although it is usually a non-GMO product, if your USP is all-natural or similar, your customers will not appreciate the addition of citric acid. Use lemon juice instead.

You could also use lime juice instead of lemon juice. However, lime juice *adds* flavor instead of *enhancing* flavor. I like to use lime juice when making mango jam or sweet cherry jam, as I enjoy the lime-fruit flavor combination. I seldom use lime juice with peaches though, as it overpowers the delicate peach flavor.

If you make quick-cooking jams, you may notice that your recipe doesn't call for added acid, even if you are making a low-acid fruit jam. This is because commercial pectin often adds acid to the pectin itself, thus eliminating that step for you.

Long-Cooking Jams vs Quick-Cooking Jams

Do you prefer long-cooking jams or quick-cooking jams? What are the advantages – and disadvantages – of each? Do particular fruits set up better when using one method over the other? Let's see!

What is Long-Cooking Jam?

You may know the long-cooking method by another name; traditional. Long cooked jams are how our grandmothers and great-grandmothers prepared soft spreads many years ago. They combined fruit, sugar, and sometimes lemon juice, brought the mixture to a slow boil, heated it up and cooked rapidly until it reached the gelling point.

Sometimes, according to location, fruit acidity, and fruit pectin level, this process took 15 minutes. Sometimes it took an hour. Usually it fell (falls) around 30-40 minutes. This is still my preferred method for making jams. Let me tell you why.

Advantages of Long-Cooking Jams

Flavor: Cooking the fruit/sugar/acid mixture for a long time leads to a more caramelized fruit flavor. I prefer this in-depth flavor. Maybe you do too!

Sugar: Less sugar is needed for long-cooking jams. Don't get me wrong, you still need to use plenty of sugar, but less than you use for other methods.

Texture: Long-cooking jams set with a softer texture than quick-cooking jams.

Disadvantages of Long Cooking Jams

Time Consuming: Long-cooking jams can be time consuming. Naturally, long-cooking jams made with high-pectin fruits like cranberries or quince will set up in a matter of minutes. But long-cooking jams made with lower pectin fruits, like most berries, could take up to an hour to gel. This is especially true if you live in a humid area or are trying to make jam on a humid day.

Gelling Point: Finding the gelling point for long-cooking jams sometimes seems like an art form. For most fruit, I have resorted to using the thermometer method. I can successfully use the cold plate method with peach or apricot jams, but struggle with this method when making berry jams. For more on gelling methods see Chapter 4.

Long-Cooking Jam Considerations

Many publications claim that you cannot make long-cooking jam using low-pectin fruits like raspberries or pears. That these low-pectin fruits require adding commercial pectin (or your own homemade pectin) to gel.

If we stop to think about this for a moment though, we realize it can't be true – at least not all the time. Our grandmothers made perfectly fine raspberry or blueberry jam without added pectin, and we can too. But since there is less pectin involved, the following become even more important:

1. Use a combination of ripe fruit and slightly under-ripe fruit. For example, it's a good idea to add some sour blueberries along with your luscious, ripe blueberries. Or chop up a green, under-ripe pear to go along with your soft, sweet pears. A ratio of ¾ ripe fruit to ¼ under-ripe fruit should be fine.
2. Add acid. It's always a good idea to add lemon juice, especially when making jam from low-acid fruits like sweet cherries, peaches, and pears. Most recipes using these fruits will call for ¼ cup of lemon juice per five or six half-pint jars of jam.

What is Quick-Cooking Jam?

Quick-cooking jam came into vogue once commercially prepared pectin became readily available. We can purchase liquid pectin and powdered pectin in most grocery stores. Commercially prepared pectin is made from either apple peel or citrus peel.

Advantages of Quick-Cooking Jams

Time-saving: Adding pectin reduces the time needed for gel to occur. Depending upon type used – liquid vs. powder – jam may set in as little as one minute.

Flavor: If you prefer a clear and pristine fruit flavor, this is the method for you. Quick-cooking jams have a flavor similar to fresh fruit since the fruit doesn't cook for very long. Instead of the rich, caramel flavor achieved with the long-cooking method, the quick-cooking method produces a bright, slightly tart flavor.

Eye-Catching: When browsing the jam aisle at a specialty foods store you can always pick out the products made by the quick-cooking method. They are the translucent, jewel-toned jams, marmalades, and preserves. Added pectin, along with the short cooking time, allows the fruit to be quickly suspended in the clear pectin. The result is usually a sparkling soft spread.

Gelling Point: Usually, there isn't a *is it set, isn't it set?* gelling point dilemma with the quick-cooking method. Once pectin is added, and the mixture is cooked following the recipe, the jam is set.

Disadvantages of Quick-Cooking Jams

Alternative Sweeteners: While a long-cooking jam adapts well to using honey or maple syrup along with sugar, a quick-cooking jam doesn't always behave as well with these alternative sweeteners. It's best to use a recipe specifically designed for added pectin and honey if you want to use an alternative sweetener.

Texture: Quick-cooking jams set up sturdier than long-cooking jams. To me, that is a disadvantage since I prefer a softer set. You may feel the exact opposite though, and consider this an advantage!

Sugar: Quick-cooking jams require adding more sugar than long-cooking jams. However, there are special types of powdered pectin available, made especially for quick-cooking low-sugar jams.

Recipes: Quick-cooking jams must be made following the recipes included with the particular type of pectin you purchase. For example, you cannot substitute liquid pectin for powdered pectin in a powdered pectin recipe – and vice versa.

Quick-Cooking Jam Considerations

Although we have been using added pectin products to make jam and other soft spreads for decades, there are still a few things you should consider before choosing this method.

1. Added pectin causes stomach upset for many people. If your child will not eat jam with their peanut butter, or you feel queasy after eating toast and jam, it may be the added pectin. Pectin is a type of fiber, and is difficult for some people to digest. You may also suffer this effect from eating gummy candy or even gummy vitamins.
2. There have been many concerns about commercially prepared pectin containing GMO products. Usually this is from the dextrose added to the pectin powder. Dextrose is most often made from corn, and most of our corn is genetically modified.

3. Commercially prepared pectin for jam is not organic. Therefore, if making organic jam is important to you, the long-cooking method is best.

Whether you choose the long-cooking method of making jam, or the quick-cooking method, your end result will be fantastic! The method you choose is personal preference, there is no right or wrong method.

How to Alter a Jam Recipe and Make It Your Own

This is most likely what started you on your jam business journey; the desire to share your creatively inspired soft spreads.

Berry Jams and Soft Spreads

Berry jams are the easiest to alter. You can substitute one type of berry for another, or even combine different kinds of berries. For example, if your blackberry jam recipe calls for 9 cups of blackberries, you can use raspberries or blueberries instead. Or, you could use 3 cups of blackberries, 3 cups of blueberries, and 3 cups of raspberries.

Stone Fruit Jams and Soft Spreads

Apricots, nectarines, peaches, and plums can also be used interchangeably. You can follow an approved apricot jam recipe but use peaches instead. Or you could combine apricots and plums. Keep in mind that apricots are softer than other stone fruit, and thus cook down more quickly.

If you are using plums or another firm stone fruit, cut it into smaller pieces before cooking.

Alternative Sweeteners

Substitute honey or maple syrup for up to one-half of the sugar in any soft spread recipe. Honey adds an almost caramel flavor to the recipe, and maple syrup adds a maple flavor. Use mild honey like wildflower or orange blossom with delicately flavored fruits like peaches or pears. More strongly flavored fruit like blackberries or cranberries are enhanced, without being overwhelmed, by maple syrup.

Adding Zest or Spices

Adding orange zest to blueberry jam or ground cinnamon to apple preserves is one of the easiest ways to turn an everyday soft spread into something extra special. You can safely add up to 2-3 teaspoons of ground spices to an approved recipe that makes eight or more half-pints of jam. Add ground spices along with all the other ingredients. You can also add whole spices in a spice bag. Be sure to remove the spice bag before spooning the jam into jars.

Citrus zest – orange, tangerine, lemon, or lime – enhances flavor and adds tanginess. Add up to 2 teaspoons of grated zest or peel to recipes that make enough for eight half-pint jars or more.

Adding Alcohol

Wine and spirits give soft spreads an intense flavor. Better yet, the alcohol evaporates during the cooking process, leaving only the flavor compounds. I usually add ¼ to ½ cup of alcohol to the cooking mixture. Spirits that work well with soft spreads are Bourbon, Rum, Kirsch, Brandy, Cognac, Port wine, Grand Marnier and Champagne or Prosecco. Keep in mind that there are strict government rules about using alcoholic beverages in your products. You will have to contact your state Liquor Control Board to obtain a liquor license.

Designing a Tasty Product

Some people love the paperwork side of running a business. Others delight in personally cooking batches of jam and watching the completed jars line up on the counter. Many find their favorite part is seeking out new markets and interacting with customers. And then there are those of us who adore designing new kinds of soft spreads.

While peach butter is wonderful, designing your own spiced peach butter is even better! As is adding another fruit to peach butter to make apricot-peach butter. Or maybe a different flavoring to create something like tangerine-peach butter. For those of us who enjoy the creative process, once we get going it can be hard to stop.

Unusually flavored soft spreads can give you a competitive advantage also. There are several ways to accomplish this:

- You could use a lesser known fruit like boysenberry or loganberry.
- Or you could add an unexpected spice like black pepper or cardamom.
- Or you could include creative flavors like rose petals or balsamic vinegar.

For example, strawberries combine well with elderflower, peach is enhanced by tarragon or lemon verbena, and oranges and mint have a natural affinity.

But adding flavors and creating new products can quickly get out of hand. We don't want to offer so many similar products that it confuses our customers. And we don't want to overwhelm our budget by requiring dozens, or even hundreds, of ingredients and newly designed and printed labels. Mostly though – don't be tempted to add too many different parts to a new product!

When we are in that creative mode, it's easy to lose perspective. If one flavoring is great, maybe two or three will be better! It's important to remember that just as too many cooks spoil the broth, too many flavorings make a muddled food product.

A few years ago, I purchased an overly-creative food product. An established sauce and condiment company rolled out their new offering, Cherry Chipotle Balsamic BBQ Sauce. While it was true that both chipotle flavoring and balsamic vinegar were wildly popular flavors, you didn't often see them together – for a reason. When the combination was added to cherry it became not the smoky-sweet flavor they were seeking, but a cloying sauce that couldn't decide if it was Mediterranean in nature or Mexican in nature. Needless to say, it wasn't on the market for very long.

Another example is an online recipe that pops up every few months for Oatmeal Raisin Peanut Butter Chocolate Chip Cookies. Oatmeal cookies are good. Oatmeal Raisin cookies are good. Oatmeal Peanut Butter cookies are good. Peanut Butter cookies are good. Peanut Butter Chocolate Chip cookies are good. But oatmeal + raisins + peanut butter + chocolate chips? Just.....no. Step away from the recipe and stop adding ingredients!

Both of these examples try to do too much, and in the end do too little. Combining so many flavors leads to a muddled product, and doesn't let any flavor shine. Customers are drawn to *all-natural*, or *artisan*, or *eat local* products because true flavor shines through. When designing a new product, use flavorings that enhance the primary taste, not cover it up. For some, determining which flavors go together is second nature – we just know without being able to explain why. But others of us need a little help. I recommend using the book *The Flavor Bible* by Karen Page and Andrew Dornenburg to help guide your product flavor combinations.

It's time to capture all of your creative product ideas. Jot them down on the following Notes page.

Will you use a pectin product for your soft spreads? If so, which type?

What kind of sugar will you use for your soft spread products? Honey? Maple Syrup? Cane sugar? Beet sugar? Capture your thoughts before you forget!

Will your product be a long-cooking product or a quick-cooking product?

Do you have any additional recipe ideas to add to your initial product offerings?

Go to **ReneePottle.com/Profitable-Preserves** to receive a PDF copy of this checklist.

Notes

CHAPTER 4

Remarkable Recipes Creating Unique Products

"Creativity involves breaking out of expected patterns in order to look at things in a different way." Edward de Bono

Some artists paint tranquil landscapes that sooth us with their beauty. Other artists capture fleeting moments with a camera lens, preserving cherished memories. Still other artists create original literature or cinema that transports us to fantastical worlds. But our artistic creations come in a jar. A jar of uniquely-flavored sparkling jam, jelly, or other soft spread. Creating luscious new products may be your favorite business task. Here are a few ideas to get you started.

Water Bath Canning Basics

Water Bath Canning is appropriate for high acid foods only.

High acid + boiling water + processing time = destruction of harmful bacteria and molds.

Most berries and fruits, most pickles, jams, jellies and other soft spreads are considered high acid foods.

1. Heat water to boiling in a tea kettle or saucepan.
2. Fill water bath canner half full of warm water, or enough water to cover jars by at least one inch of water. Heat to 140 – 180 degrees.
3. Add ¼ cup of white vinegar to canner. The vinegar keeps jars bright and shiny and also slows canner rack rusting.
4. Use clean canning jars, lids, and rings that have been washed in the dishwasher, if your recipe processing time is at least 10 minutes.
5. Alternatively, use jars sterilized for 10 minutes in boiling water. Jars MUST be sterilized if your recipe processing time is less than 10 minutes, (e.g. jelly). If using sterilized jars, lids and rings must also be sterilized in boiling water.
6. Fill jars leaving recommended amount of head space. Most jams call for ¼ inch head space.
7. Wipe jar lips with a clean damp cloth or paper towel.
8. Place lids on filled jars.
9. Hand tighten rings on jars. Don't over – tighten!
10. Load filled jars into the canner rack. Conversely, if your canner rack is already in the canner, load jars into the rack using a jar lifter.
11. Place canner rack and jars in canner. Make sure water is 1 – 2 inches over top of jars. If not, add boiling water started in Step 1.

12. Bring water to a boil. Cover, turn down heat slightly (it must remain boiling) and process for recipe recommended length of time.
13. When processing time is complete; turn off burner, carefully remove cover, and remove jars using a jar lifter. DO NOT tip jars to displace water on lids. The water will evaporate.
14. Place hot jars on a towel to cool. Let sit for 12 to 24 hours.

Congratulations! You are now a Water Bath Canning Pro. Remember, repetition will make this process easier each time. Enjoy your bounty of safe, delicious, home canned goods.

Determining the Gelling Point

The jam gelling point, also called jam set, is when your soft spread reaches the perfect consistency; not too runny and not too thick.

Making jam or jelly with prepared pectin is usually straightforward and simple. Add the pectin, bring to a boil, boil for two minutes and voila! Perfectly prepared jam.

Using the natural pectin in long-cooking jams though, requires a bit more finesse. Don't worry, it still isn't a difficult process and the little bit of extra work is worth the added flavor.

There are several different methods to check for the gelling point. Use whichever one of these methods work best for you.

Plate Method

I used this method for decades with excellent results. Drop some of the cooking jam onto a glass plate and put it in the refrigerator for a minute. If the jam sets up to the level you like (there is no such thing as the "right" level, only the level you prefer) remove the cooking jam from the heat and ladle it into jars.

Cold Plate Method

Similar to above, cool a glass plate in the freezer until it is cold, usually just a minute or two. Drop some of the cooking jam onto the plate. Draw a spoon through the jam. If the line stays separated, the jam is set.

Spoon or Sheet Method

Using a metal spoon, stir the cooking jam and then lift it out of the mixture. If the jam falls off the spoon in a sheet, it has successfully thickened. It may be difficult for you to correctly judge the thickness if you are new to jam making. I also find berry jams difficult to judge this way and end up over cooking them.

Temperature Method

This method is the easiest, with a caveat. Jam is usually set when the temperature reaches eight to nine degrees above the temperature of boiling water. Water usually boils at 212 degrees Fahrenheit, but not always. Several things can affect the temperature, including altitude and barometric pressure.

If you use this method, check today's boiling water temperature first. Otherwise you may end up with burnt jam from cooking too long.

The above sections are reprinted from the author's cookbook, *Creative Jams and Preserves.*

Determine the Best-By Date

Check any commercially canned or bottled food product, and you will find a *best-by* date. This means that, according to the manufacturer, the product will taste best if used before the listed date. A best-by date refers to product *quality*, not product *safety*. Best-by dates are usually found on shelf stable or frozen food items, like canned vegetables, frozen fruit, peanut butter, and jams, jellies and other soft spreads.

The best-by date is not the same as an expiration date. An expiration date means that the product is not safe to eat after the listed date. You will find an expiration date on most packaged deli foods and items from the dairy case.

If properly made and processed, and the seal has not broken, your soft spreads should be safe for years. But flavor and color quality will deteriorate after a year or two. Best-by dates identify *quality*. Most soft spreads retain quality for one-two years.

Apricot Jam Recipe

8 cups chopped, slightly crushed, pitted apricots
¼ cup lemon juice
6 cups granulated sugar
9 (half-pint) jars and lids

1. Add the apricots, sugar, and lemon juice to a large Dutch oven.
2. Slowly bring the mixture to a boil over medium heat, stirring until the sugar is dissolved.
3. Turn the heat up a little and cook rapidly, stirring often to prevent sticking, until the jam reaches the gelling point, about 25 minutes.
4. Spoon hot jam into prepared jars, leaving ¼ inch head space.
5. Wipe the lip of each jar with a damp paper towel, top the jars with a lid and a lid ring.
6. Process the jars in a water bath canner for 15 minutes. Remove and let cool completely.

Apricot Jam Variations

Use your creativity to turn a basic apricot jam recipe into something unique:

Raspberry-Apricot Jam: Combine 7 cups of raspberries with 2 cups of chopped apricots. Delete the lemon juice, and then follow the above cooking directions.

Apricot Amaretto Jam: Add ½-1 cup of Amaretto to step 2 above, then continue with cooking directions.

Peach/Nectarine/Plum/Mango Jam: Replace the apricots with the same amount of peeled, chopped peaches, nectarines, plums, or mango.

Apricot Orange Jam: Add the zest from one large orange at step 3.

Spiced Apricot Jam: Add 1-2 teaspoons of ground cardamom at step 2.

Berry Jam: Replace the chopped apricots with 9 cups of blueberries, raspberries, strawberries, blackberries, or some combination of berries. Delete the lemon juice. Makes about 8 (half-pint) jars.

Apple Jelly Recipe

4 cups apple juice (from 3-4 pounds of apples)
3 cups granulated sugar
4 (half-pint) jars and lids

1. Pour juice into a large pot. Add sugar.
2. Stir to dissolve sugar.
3. Bring to a boil over high heat, stirring constantly.

4. Cook and stir until jelly has set; usually at eight degrees above boiling water temperature or about 220 degrees.
5. Or, use the sheet test method to determine if the jelly has set.
6. Remove from heat, skim foam if necessary.
7. Ladle into sterilized jars leaving ¼ inch head space.
8. Process in a water bath canner for 5 minutes

Apple Jelly Variations

Remember, you usually cannot make no-pectin added jelly with commercial juice. This is because the pectin is broken down during the pasteurization process and filtered out. When making jelly, either use a pectin-added recipe or make your own juice from tart apples, grapes, or quince.

Apple Plum Jelly: Use 3 cups apple juice and 1 cup red plum juice, then follow directions as written.

Apple Berry Jelly: Use 2 cups apple juice and 2 cups berry juice.

Grape Jelly: Use 4 cups of Concord grape juice instead of apple juice.

Peach Plum Jelly: Use 1 1/3 cups each of peach juice, plum juice, and apple juice.

Apple Kirsch Jelly: Add 1/3 cup of Kirsch to step 2 above.

Lemon Jelly: Use 4 cups of homemade lemon juice instead of apple juice.

Quince Jelly: Use 4 cups of quince juice instead of apple juice.

Spiced Jelly: Infuse fruit juice by adding a cinnamon stick, whole spices, a vanilla bean, or sprig of basil, rosemary, or lemon verbena to fruit when making juice for jelly. Remove the whole spices or herbs and then continue with recipe as written.

Peach Preserves Recipe

8 cups peeled, sliced peaches (about 10 large peaches)
6 cups granulated sugar
7 (half-pint) jars and lids

1. Combine peaches and sugar in a large bowl.
2. Cover and let sit in the refrigerator for 12-18 hours.
3. Transfer the fruit/sugar combination to a large saucepan.
4. Bring slowly to a boil over medium heat. Stir frequently to prevent scorching.
5. Boil gently until the fruit becomes clear and the syrup thickens, about 40 minutes.
6. Use the plate method to check for gelling or use a digital thermometer. Gelling is reached at 220 degrees or eight degrees above the boiling point of water.
7. Spoon the hot preserves into prepared jars, leaving ¼ inch head space.
8. Wipe the lip of each jar with a damp paper towel, top the jars with a lid and a lid ring.

9. Process the jars in a water bath canner for 15 minutes. Remove and let cool completely.

Peach Preserves Variations

Use any fruit that can hold its shape to make preserves. Some berries, like blueberries or currants, make lovely preserves. Berries that cook down, like strawberries or raspberries, are better suited to jam.

Honey Peach Preserves: Use 3 cups of granulated sugar and 3 cups of honey in the above recipe.

Plum Preserves: Use 8 cups of chopped, pitted plums instead of peaches. Plums do not have to be peeled.

Cherry Preserves: Instead of peaches, use 4 pounds of pitted, sour cherries. Add 3 Tablespoons of lemon juice at step 4. The sour cherry/sugar combination only has to sit for 1 hour instead of 12 hours.

Blueberry Preserves: Combine 4 pounds of blueberries and the sugar. Slowly bring to a boil over medium heat. Reduce heat, simmer for 5 minutes, remove from heat, and let sit for 12-18 hours. Continue above directions starting with step 3 above.

Spirited Preserves: Add up to 1 cup of alcohol spirits at step 3 above. Use spirits that enhance the fruit flavor like; blueberries + Cointreau, plums + port wine, apples + rum, or nectarines + tequila.

Apple Butter Recipe

4 pounds apples
2 cups water
4 cups sugar
2 teaspoons ground cinnamon
6 (half-pint) jars and lids

1. Wash apples. Core but do not peel. Cut into small pieces.
2. Place in a large pot with water. Cook over low heat until soft. Cool to almost room temperature.
3. Purée apples and liquid in a blender or food processor or using an immersion blender.
4. Measure purée.
5. Return purée to pot - you should have about 8 cups of purée. Add sugar and cinnamon.
6. Cook over medium-low heat, stirring often until mixture has thickened.
7. Ladle into hot, clean jars leaving about ¼ inch head space. Top with the two-piece lids and rings, and process in a water bath for 10 minutes.

Apple Butter Variations

Fruit Butters are the easiest soft spread to prepare. There is no concern about reaching the gelling point, as the mixture is thickened by cooking out the extra liquid. However, this is a longer cooking process than making jam or preserves.

Peach or Pear Butter: Follow the above directions using pitted peaches or pears instead of apples. Eliminate the ground cinnamon if desired.

Cherry Almond Butter: Use 5-6 pounds sweet cherries instead of apples. Don't forget to pit the cherries first! Add 2 teaspoons almond extract instead of ground cinnamon.

Spiced Pear Butter: Use chopped pears instead of apples. Substitute 1 teaspoon ground ginger and ¼ teaspoon ground cloves for the ground cinnamon.

Maple Apple Butter: Follow the above recipe using 2 cups of granulated sugar and 2 cups of maple syrup.

Paradise Butter: Use a combination of quince, tart apple, and cranberries equaling 4 pounds. Eliminate the cinnamon.

Stone Fruit Butter: Use a combination of mango, peach, apricot, and nectarines instead of apples – enough to make 8 cups of purée. Eliminate the ground cinnamon and add ¼ cup lime juice.

Berry Butter: Use a combination of strawberries, raspberries, and blackberries instead of apples – enough to make 8 cups of purée. Reduce water to 1 cup, and eliminate cinnamon. Put cooked mixture through a food mill in step 3 to remove seeds. Continue as directed.

Have these recipes inspired additional creative ideas?

Let's capture those thoughts!

Will you add citrus zest or an herb infusion to your soft spread? If so, which?

Will you add a spiced soft spread to your product line?

Will you use ground spices? Whole spices?

Will you combine two (or more) different fruits in any of your products? Which combinations are you considering?

Go to **ReneePottle.com/Profitable-Preserves** to receive a PDF copy of this checklist.

Notes

CHAPTER 5

The Professional Perspective Make Your Business Legal in 7 Easy Steps

"If you don't build your dream, someone will hire you to help build theirs." Tony Gaskins, Dream Chaser

Now that you have determined what you will make and sell, it's almost time to make jam! But first, let's take care of necessary business legal requirements. These requirements may appear overwhelming, but don't worry – just follow them step-by-step and soon you will be a proud business owner bringing in cash!

Step 1: Name Your Business

Several years ago, I read a story about the actress Barbara Hershey. Apparently, in the heady hippie days, she named her son, Free. At some point he asked her what "Free" meant. She told him, "It means you are free to change your name anytime you want." He chose Tom as his new name.

I have no idea if that story is true, nonetheless it raises a good point; when naming a business, much like naming a book or a baby or even a pet, your initial idea might not be the best long-term option. Keep the following in mind as you brainstorm potential business names:

Specific

Your business deserves a name specific enough that customers understand what you do (*Jenny's Homemade Delights*), but not so specific that it limits your business and stifles growth (not *Jenny's Homemade Strawberry Jam*).

Puns

Don't be tempted to use a pun as your business name. Surprisingly many people don't understand puns. It may seem funny and memorable to you, but leaves others confused. You don't want anyone to be confused about your business! So, while I think *In a Jam* is a fantastic business name, many people don't understand the pun.

Clever

For the same reason, don't use something that you see as clever for a business name. As a rule, most people don't really want to stop and think about something. If they have to puzzle out your name they may move on to the next business.

Offensive

Avoid choosing a name that some might find offensive. Using *bleeped out* words or titles is quite popular these days, but many find this offensive. Usually we don't want to discourage potential customers, but this is exactly what happens when your business has an offensive name. Some people won't even taste your products if they are offended by the name. Choose something a little less offensive. You might consider the name boring, but a boring business name that attracts customers is preferable to an offensive name that repels customers!

Obscure

Likewise, avoid giving your business a name with an obscure connection. It may have no meaning whatsoever to most people. I made this mistake with my business name, Hestia's Hearth LLC. Do you have any idea who Hestia's was? No, I didn't think so. Surprisingly, many people aren't familiar with the word Hearth either. So, my business name hit the bad decision jackpot; combining an obscure reference and an apparently uncommon noun. I made this mistake so you don't have to.

Spelling

Choosing a name that is easy to spell is also preferable. It will be easier for future customers to find your business when searching online if it adheres to conventional spelling guidelines. So, don't be tempted to use the Middle English *The Preserven Company*, when you really want *The Preserves Company*. Few of your customers will be Middle English experts. Most of us have no idea what a *Preserven* is.

Lyrical

Make sure your chosen name has a pleasant sound. One way to do so is to use alliteration (I got this part right with Hestia's Hearth LLC). Alliteration is two or more words that start with the same sound, for example, *Jenny's Jam*, or *Sophisticated Soft Spreads*. Most of us are attracted to the poetic rhythm that alliteration lends. If you are using alliteration, keep your business name short. More than three alliterative words and your business name goes from musical to a tongue twister. *Jenny's Genuine Jamaican Jams*, anyone?

•

This is a good time to purchase your business domain name also, even if you don't plan to set up a website right away. A dot com (.com) domain is most desired. It's always best if your business name and your domain match. For this reason, you may want to come up with 3 or 4 prospective business name options, and check to see which corresponding domain name is available.

Just because there isn't a website attached to your desired domain name, doesn't mean that the name isn't already registered. Go to whois.com to find out if your desired business name is available.

> *Are you struggling to come up with a business name? Don't worry. Just like baby-naming books and websites, there are tools to help you choose a great business name too. Try Dot-o-mator, a business naming tool. (www.dotomator.com)*

What if you have your heart set on JoeSchmoeCopperKettle.com, but it is owned by someone else? You have a few choices:

- You could contact the owner and see if they are willing to sell the domain name.
- You could use an available extension like .biz or .net, although recognize that if you do this many prospective customers will try the .com address first.
- You could slightly change the domain name, like from JoeSchmoeCopperKettle to JoeSchmoeCopperKettles, but many prospective customers will inadvertently go to JoeSchmoeCopperKettle.com (the singular Kettle instead of the plural Kettles) first.
- You could change it a little more, maybe to JoesCopperKettle or TheCopperKettle. This change might work, plus it eliminates the difficult to spell Schmoe.
- Or you could go in a different direction altogether and forget Joe, Schmoe, Copper, and Kettle for something like PapasKitchen or SweetSpreads.

However, if your heart is set on Joe Schmoe Copper Kettle, remember it's *your* business. You really can name it whatever you want, as long as you don't infringe on someone else's trademark or break any laws. Perhaps your jams will be so unique that the clunky name becomes an advantage. Or maybe you will devise a creative promotional plan that goes viral, putting your business name on everyone's lips. However, attracting customers is usually easier if your name is easy to remember.

You may want to trademark your business name. A trademark is basically a brand name. Once your trademark is registered, no one in the same or a related business can use the same name. For most people with a small jam business, going through the trademark process is an unnecessary expense, especially when just starting out. But we don't want to be sued for infringing on someone else's trademark, so search the Trademark Electronic Search System and make sure your proposed name is not already trademarked by someone else.

Step 2: Choose Your Business Entity Type

Despite the desire to just start making and selling jam, you should choose a business entity type before selling any product. Choosing a business entity keeps you out of legal trouble (most states don't look kindly on people selling food illegally), and allows you to earn the tax advantages that come with owning your own business – even if it is a micro-sized business! You will probably want to choose one of the following types:

Sole Proprietorship

As a sole proprietor, you are the single owner of your business. Many small businesses start out this way, because it is the simplest of all legal entities. Being a sole proprietor requires no additional legal forms beyond the business licenses, and a DBA (doing business as) form that identifies your business name.

A DBA form lets your business legally operate under a name other than your own. (DBA stands for *Doing Business As*.) For example, maybe your business name is Joe Schmoe Enterprises, yet you make jam under the Joe Schmoe Copper Kettle name. A DBA form clarifies that the latter name is actually part of the former business.

Who cares? Surprisingly, lots of people. Let's say I purchased some of your jam, and wrote a check to Joe Schmoe Copper Kettle because that is the name on your label. If you don't have a DBA form your bank won't let you deposit, or cash, the check. Why? Because your business name is Joe Schmoe Enterprises, not Joe Schmoe Copper Kettle. Banks used to be much more relaxed about this problem, but the 2008 banking crisis resulted in stricter guidelines. Your town/municipality may require a DBA as a separate form, or it may be rolled in with your local business license.

However, as a sole proprietor you are personally liable if there is a problem with your product. This means you personally can be sued and your personal assets can be seized to cover your liability. I do not recommend this entity type, especially when working with food.

Partnership

In a partnership, you own your business with one or more other individuals. The conventional wisdom of forming a partnership waxes and wanes. For many years forming a partnership was discouraged, as partners have a tendency to disagree on the future direction of the business, sometimes causing personal and financial hardships.

Current thought though, is that partnerships combine the best skills of two or more people, giving the business an advantage over a single owner.

A partnership is a simple business entity, similar to a sole proprietorship. However, you and your partners are personally liable if there is an issue, just as with a sole proprietorship.

To form a partnership, you must register your partnership name with your state licensing agency and File a DBA form.

LLC (Limited Liability Company)

Each state has slightly different LLC rules, but the following generalities are true for all. This is the format I usually recommend for food related businesses.

A Limited Liability Company combines the tax and liability advantages of a corporation with the flexibility of a partnership. It is less expensive to create than creating a traditional corporation. While the business (or LLC) can be sued, the individual owners (called members) are not held personally liable.

Establishing an LLC is a lengthier process than creating a sole proprietorship or partnership, and costs more too. Members must pay self-employment taxes on any profit, but the income gained can go through your personal taxes.

Although you may be able to set up a LLC by yourself, following directions on your state licensing site, you could also choose to hire a lawyer or tax professional to do this for you. LLC registration costs vary in each state, but are usually in the $200 range. Note – even if you create an LLC, you will most likely also need a business license, either a state license or a local license or both.

Many states also require that you provide annual meeting notes, or an online statement showing that your LLC remains in good standing. You may also have to draw up Articles of Operation/Organization - but don't panic. These articles don't have to be very complicated for a small jam business. I have listed some free template resources in Chapter 9.

Find out the specific LLC requirements for your location by searching your state Department of Licensing website.

S-Corp

An S-Corp is a type of corporation that is more complex than an LLC but less complex than a traditional C-corporation.

While a C-corporation is taxed as a separate entity, a S-corporation is not taxed, allowing the profits to flow through to owner's (shareholders) personal taxes.

However, a S-Corp is more expensive and more complex to set up than a sole proprietorship, partnership, or LLC. Strict record keeping for governmental purposes is required and you will definitely want to enlist the services of both an accountant and a lawyer for this legal entity.

For most cottage or small (micro) businesses setting up an S-Corp is unnecessary. I recommend that you set up a simple LLC, following the directions on your state's licensing site for your business. If at some point your business grows into a larger, full-time business, you may want to convert your LLC to an S-Corp.

Step 3: Get Your Licenses and Certifications

You are probably frustrated at hearing this again, but as with LLC regulations, each state/municipality has differing rules about what you need for licenses. The resources section in Chapter 9 will help you sort out what you need for your state. Start with a state government Google.com search, and call your local town hall for local advice. These are licenses that you may need:

Town or Municipality

Some towns or municipalities require a local license. This is especially true when working from your home. Not all types of businesses can be operated from all neighborhoods. For example, while I can legally operate a day care or a digital publishing business from my home, I cannot operate a boutique from my home, as my neighborhood is not zoned for commercial traffic.

State License (Master License)

Sometime you may need both a local and a state business license. Contact your state Department of Licensing or visit it online to see if this pertains to you.

Reseller's License

If you plan to sell your products wholesale, you may need a reseller license too. This can usually be found on your state Department of Licensing website. A reseller's license is different from a master license. The *master* license shows that your business is legal to work in your state. A *reseller's* license lets you sell your products to someone else who then sells them to the final customer. A reseller's license means you don't collect sales tax on the products you sell wholesale. This license also lets you purchase soft spread ingredients and packaging materials without paying sales tax. Find more on wholesale sales versus retail sales in Chapter 7.

Department of Agriculture (State)

Canned jams and soft spreads regulations usually fall under your state Department of Agriculture rules. You will probably need a food manufacturer/processor license or a cottage food license in addition to the above licenses.

Health Department (Local)

In most states, local health agencies focus on companies that prepare and serve food, like caterers, instead of those who process food, like soft spread manufacturers. Exceptions to this rule may occur when you are serving samples at a craft show or farmer's market. In these instances, you may need a temporary health department license. Don't wait until the last minute to apply! It may take a little time to pull everything together. For example, in my local area the health department requires a hand wash station. I have successfully met this requirement by using a large water container with a spout, setting it up in a corner of the display area, using a dish basin or bucket to let the water run and using antibacterial soap. Your state/area may have a similar requirement.

If you operate a cottage industry you will have even more contact with the local health department. In many states, health department technicians assure safety compliance by inspecting your home kitchen.

EIN

If you plan to hire employees, or you register as an LLC or S-Corp, you must apply for a federal EIN (Employee Identification Number) for tax purposes.

You can apply for your EIN online through the www.irs.gov site. Type EIN into the search box to be directed to the information page. You can also apply via mail.

There may be some confusion over filing for an EIN. Even if you don't have employees you still need an EIN. I found this out the hard way when I switched my sole proprietorship to an LLC. I had no employees, and didn't even pay myself. So, when I called my state licensing agency, they assured me that I didn't need an EIN. Unfortunately. the federal government felt differently and levied a fine on my business. It was a costly mistake that required the help of a Certified Public Accountant to rectify. Save yourself the hassle and the extra cash and get an EIN number!

Food Handler's Card

Most states require some sort of food handler's certification to work with food. The certification usually consists of a 1-4-hour class followed by a short exam. Contact your local Health Department to find out the requirements for your area.

Step 4: Set Up a Bank Account

Many years ago, I taught high school sophomores how to balance a checkbook. I know, seems quaint now, doesn't it? But in the days before computers, if you wanted to know how much money was in your account, you had to keep track of your income and expenses. Just because you still had checks, didn't mean you had money. Running a business is like personal finance was in the *good old days*. You still need to record incoming and outgoing payments.

The easiest way to do this is to keep your personal banking separate from your business banking.

Set up a business checking account: Start with your local bank as it's always a good idea to have a personal relationship with your business bank. No doubt, they will be happy to set up another account for you. You can also seek out and compare other bank or credit union options, as their business accounts may be less expensive.

Get a business credit card if possible: Sometimes you can do this through your bank, other times it is next to impossible to get a business credit card until you have a business track record. If you are not able to get a business credit card, I recommend setting aside a personal credit card that is used only for business. That way it is easier to keep your business and personal expenses separate.

Step 5: How Will You Accept Payment?

If you only plan to sell at Farmer's markets or craft events you may be able to accept cash only. But since most people carry little cash these days it is best to accept credit and debit cards. Luckily this is easier than ever. Not that many years ago you had to have a credit card merchant account, but today there are many more options.

PayPal® or Google Wallet

These online payment options make sending payment, receiving payment, and sending invoices safe and easy.

There is no need to have a credit card merchant account or to worry about online security as customer payments go through the PayPal® or Google Wallet sites, not your website. Find more information at PayPal®.com and Google.com.

Square

This is the best service for accepting credit card payments from anywhere. You no longer need to be tethered to a phone line or electrical cord. Attach the Square equipment to your phone or tablet, and process payments through the Square app. Find all the information you need at Squareup.com.

Bank merchant account

This is the old-fashioned way to accept payment. It is still a useful method, because you have more control over both security and payment methods. However, merchant accounts are more expensive and more time consuming to set up than either PayPal® or Google Wallet. To set up a merchant account, talk to your bank. They will have the necessary forms. Even if you start your business using Square, you may switch to a merchant account once the business has grown, and you are accepting several large orders each month. The cost of a merchant account becomes more reasonable as order volume increases.

I recommend starting your business with a PayPal® or Google Wallet account for online payments, and Square for mobile payments. Once your business has grown, you may want to add your own merchant account.

Step 6: Don't Forget Insurance

Ah yes, the need for insurance. The bane of modern-day living. You definitely need liability insurance for protection, in case something goes wrong with a product and someone is hurt. An inexpensive business insurance rider can often be added to your home or renter's insurance policy. Ask your insurance company if they provide this service. If not, you will need to find a new insurance company, one that specializes in working with small businesses.

How much insurance coverage should you have? According to specialists at Harvey Insurance in Pasco, Washington, you should have no less than $1 million in liability coverage, with a $2 million aggregate policy. Of course, this number can change based on whether you work from home, rent space in a food incubator, or build your own commercial kitchen. The policy should protect you from any foodborne illness or property damage.

Do shop around, and don't feel stuck with the first quote you receive. My first business insurance cost estimate was for $5000 annually. The policy I ended up purchasing cost $500/year. Huge difference.

Step 7: The Rules About Labeling

Labeling rules vary with business size. Don't worry, by starting small you won't need the same in-depth label that you see in the grocery store. But you will need a label that meets standard requirements. There are lots of companies who will expertly make your labels, or you can make your own simple label using a home printer.

Cottage Industry Statement

Most states require a cottage industry statement that the product has been made in a home kitchen. For example, "*This product was produced under the Washington State Cottage Food Law in a home kitchen,*" or something similar. The statement can go on the front or the back label, but must be in large enough font to be easily seen!

Business Name and Address

No matter which type of business you operate, a cottage industry business or a small food processor business, federal guidelines specify that the manufacturer's physical address, not a post office box address, be printed on the label. Although some states only require a company website address, most follow the federal rules and demand the entire address.

You might consider this requirement a disadvantage when following cottage food laws, as your home address will be listed on your product labels. For some people this isn't a detriment. Others though, consider it an invasion of privacy.

For small food manufacturers/processors, the label must indicate the name of your business and where the product is manufactured. For example, if you make your soft spreads at a rented commercial kitchen, the label would include that address. If you have your own offsite manufacturing facility, that is the address included on the label. If your product is manufactured by a co-packer, both the co-packer name and address would be included on the label. You may also want your business mailing address printed on the label. You can use a United States Post Office Box, or some other mail service like UPS stores or FedEx stores for your mailing address, or include your business website address instead.

Product Name

Making Peach Butter? Then the label should read *Peach Butter*. Want to call it *Famous Peach Butter* or *Double Peach Butter*? Go for it. The label still correctly identifies the product; peach butter. What if you want to call it *Peach Spread*? That will probably meet guidelines too, as peach butter certainly is a peach spread. But you can't call the product *Plum Butter*, because plums and peaches are different fruits. If you purchased a jar of something called plum butter, you would expect it to contain plum butter, not peach butter.

What if you want to give your peach butter a name like *Peach Goodness in a Jar*? You absolutely can do so, BUT, you must also include the words *Peach Butter* on the label, to correctly identify the product. This seems like a nitpicky rule but it actually protects both you as the peach butter creator, and your customer. No one wants to spend their hard-earned money on something, only to open it up and find that it's not what they expected. Unpleasant surprises lead to irritated customers. No small business wants irritated customers. So, give your fantastic peach butter any name you want, but make sure the label also correctly identifies that the jar actually contains *Peach Butter*.

Ingredients

Ingredients must be listed in order of weight. For example, your peach jam may include sugar, peaches, and lemon juice. Which ingredient weighs the most? The peaches, or the sugar? It all depends upon your individual recipe, so if the peaches weigh more the ingredient list will read peaches, sugar, lemon juice. Of course, if you make Spiced Peach Jam, the ingredients list will also include *spices*. You do not have to list individual spices; thus, you can keep your recipe a trade secret. Additional ingredients need only be listed as spices, flavorings, and/or colorings unless they are an identified allergen.

Net Volume or Net Weight

Include the net weight of the finished product in both U.S. and metric units. If your jar of peach jam weighs 16 ounces, the label must also include the weight in grams – 453 grams.

Remember, net weight is the weight of the actual product, and does not include the packaging. So, the net weight of a jar of jam is ONLY the jam itself. The gross weight would be the jam plus the jar and lid and label. There is no need to include gross weight on the label.

Allergens

Federal allergen statement rules are stringent. There are eight food allergens and two additive allergens that must be identified on the label in the United States. They are: milk, egg, fish, shellfish, tree nuts (must list specific nuts), wheat, peanuts, soybeans, sulfites, and FD&C Yellow 5. If any of these ingredients are included in your products, they must be identified in both the ingredient list and as a separate statement. The statement must be in a readable font and size. The statement, for example *This product contains milk and macadamia nuts*, can be placed on the front or back label.

Nutrition Label

Nutrition labels are the labels that let us know if a product is a healthy food, or a less-healthy food. They look fancy and difficult to make, but don't worry, you will most likely be exempt from this requirement while your business remains small.

According to the Food and Drug Administration (FDA), if you sell fewer than 10,000 units annually no nutrition label is required. Additionally, if you sell more than 10,000 units but fewer than 100,000 units, and you have fewer than 10 full-time employees, you are also exempt, as long as you file an annual FDA exemption notice.

Once you have grown larger, there are specific nutritional label design guidelines that even specify the font size. Your products will also be analyzed by a food testing lab to determine the nutritive amounts. The easiest way to include a nutrition label is to have the company that analyses the jam also make the nutrition label and send it to you as an image file. That way you can include it on your label, without having to do all the design work yourself.

If you do include a nutrition label, be careful about making nutrition claims. We often read news reports about companies who *voluntarily* remove statements like *heart-healthy*, or *lowers blood sugar* from their labels. Nutrition claims must meet specific governmental guidelines. Of course, jams and other soft spreads seldom claim to *heal your gut* or *help build muscle* but it's best to completely avoid all product nutrition claims.

UPC Labels

Almost every item you purchase has a bar code, called a UPC label, attached. A UPC label helps the store owner digitally keep track of inventory and sales. If you sell your product retail only, in other words, if you plan to only sell at Farmers' Markets, Craft Fairs, Bazaars, Etsy, and your own online store, you absolutely do not need a UPC label.

If you sell wholesale to small grocery chains, gift shops, and other similar stores, you still may not need a UPC label. Larger grocery chains usually require UPC labels for all of their stocked items. However, you can wait and add this label once your business has grown, you do not need to have a UPC label in the beginning – and maybe never.

UPC codes are distributed through GS 1 (gs1us.org). The initial fee is based on the number of barcodes you need, and is currently anywhere from $250 for up to 10 barcodes, to $10,500 for up to 100,000 bar codes. There is also an annual renewal fee.

Designing Labels

Product labels are a must. Luckily there are many cost-effective options available If you are at all crafty or artistic, you can design your own label

Print labels on your home printer using Avery® or other brand labels found at office supply stores. This type of label is fine for when you are starting out and only selling via retail, like at the farmer's market, but they don't hold up to packing or long-term use. Use a simple word processing program and copyright-free clip art to create your label design.

You can also order short run labels made from several companies. These labels usually have a professional finish, and can be as fancy or plain as you like. Several short run label companies are listed in Chapter 9.

Larger quantities of labels, 1000 or more, are often more cost effective when ordered directly from a printer.

Or you can use a combination; maybe you will choose to print less expensive back ingredient labels on your home printer. Then you can order brightly colored, professionally designed and printed product labels for the front of your jars.

However, if you have no interest or talent for designing product labels, have a graphic designer do this for you.

Find low cost graphic designers at fiverr.com or check out your local college and high school programs. Professors are often looking for real-world projects for their students.

> *Include your USP key words like Old-Fashioned or Made from Local Ingredients on your label. This is exactly where you want to include what makes your product unique. The front label is like a front door, we want it to stand out and be noticed.*

One Label or Two? Generic or Specific?

Due to print-on-demand and digital printing services, label printing costs have decreased tremendously over the past few years, although they can still be a large investment. Don't disregard a label's importance, as a label is your product's front door. Much like a book cover advertises the book, your soft spread label sets the mood for your product. You want it to be attractive, welcoming, and reflect your business personality.

Consider these four options when choosing your perfect label:

One Label: You can put everything on one label. Your business name, product name, address, ingredients, and weight may fit nicely on a front label. This will reduce expenses, as you only have to pay for one label, not two labels for each product. Don't forget to use the *Made in a home kitchen* statement if necessary.

Two Labels: Of course, you may choose the standard two labels created for each product. A front label that includes your business name, product name, and weight, plus a back label that includes your business address, ingredient list, allergen statement if necessary, home kitchen statement if necessary, and optional nutrition information.

Product Specific Label: We tend to think of labels as being product specific and that your three initial products will each have their own label. For example, you will need a label for your Peach Butter, a different label for your Peach Preserves, and another for your Peach Syrup. Each of these products also needs an individual back label listing the ingredients in order of weight. Individual product labels look professional.

But it also means that you will have to have three or six different labels printed for your initial product offerings. This may work out well, but what if customers don't want Peach Preserves? Now you have a whole roll of Peach Preserve labels, but no longer make peach preserves because it doesn't sell. Is there a way to avoid the expense when trying out new products?

Joe Schmoe Copper Kettle

Product Name

Artisan Soft Spreads

1234 South Street
Anywhere, USA
JoeSchmoeCopperKettle.com

Generic Front Label

Joe Schmoe Copper Kettle
Artisan Soft Spreads

Ingredients:
Peach Butter: Fresh Peaches, Cane Sugar
Peach Preserves: Fresh Peaches, Cane Sugar
Spiced Peach Butter: Fresh Peaches, Cane Sugar, Spices

Net Weight: 8 ounces (227 grams)

Made in a facility that processes nuts

Multiple Product Back Label

Generic Labels: There are a few less costly ways to effectively label your products, especially while you are still testing which products to include in your product line. You can have a generic front label designed, and/or a generic back label designed. Your front label may include your business name and then leave a space for the product name and weight.

Your generic back label may include the business address, and leave a space for the ingredient list and allergen statement.

Then you can print out smaller labels on your own computer that include the necessary information, and attach it to the generic labels.

You can also create a multi-product back label. Have one label printed that includes the ingredients for all three of your initial products.

I recommend using a generic label for the jar fronts, one that you can use on all spreads. It may include: company name, USP, and even contact information. Leave a space so that you can add a smaller, product specific label on top.

Time to review and update your ideas!

I bet you have several business name ideas already! Write them down so you don't forget. Then check the whois.com site. Chapter 9 lists several places to purchase your desired website domain name.

What kind of legal entity will work best for you? If it is a partnership or multi-member LLC, who else will be part of your business?

What licenses do you need? Where will you find the information needed? Add pertinent phone numbers and website addresses to your to-do list now.

Where will you get a business checking account? Will you try to obtain a business credit card? Or will you designate a personal card strictly for business purposes? Write it down now to keep track.

How will you accept payment? Set up your accounts now so you are ready to receive money!

Go to **ReneePottle.com/Profitable-Preserves** to receive a PDF copy of this checklist.

Notes

CHAPTER 6

Spotlight on the Details Which Materials Do You Need?

"Hot crumpets with butter and jam – what could be more ambrosial?" William Boyd, Any Human Heart

Before you can make money, you have to make jam. And before you can make jam, you need supplies! Where will you get the necessary ingredients and equipment to make your products?

Ingredients

Luckily, soft spreads require only a few ingredients; fruit, sugar, and perhaps an additional flavoring and pectin. Fewer ingredients mean less up-front expense than many other food businesses require, but you will still have some items to purchase.

Fruit

Where will you get the fruit for your soft spreads? One wonderful thing about making jam is that the fruit does not have to be beautiful, just good quality. You don't need to purchase the most expensive, blemish-free peaches to make peach butter. Small, wind-scarred peaches may not be visually appealing in the produce bin, but they cook up into a delicious soft spread just the same.

Fresh fruit can be frozen to use later, perhaps when the weather isn't quite so warm. Wash, peel, and cut today's abundant harvest, but freeze it to use when the winter winds have set in – and fresh peaches are few and far between! Package frozen fruit in batch-size containers. So, if your peach preserves batch uses 6 pounds of peaches, freeze the fresh fruit in 6-pound amounts. Thus, saving yourself time when cooking.

Whether you are making strawberry jam, grape jelly, or blueberry preserves, a steady supply of fruit is necessary. Luckily, we have several options.

- **Grow your own**: Do you live on a large farm full of apricot trees, or have a couple of prolific peach trees in your urban backyard? Growing your own fruit is a wonderful way to start a business. In fact, excess fruit is often the reason we start a jam/jelly business. Most of us can't stand seeing perfectly good fruit going unused.
- **Local farmer or farmer's market**: If you don't grow your own fruit, look locally for someone who does! Perhaps there is a farmer's market vendor who would love to sell you cases of apples every year. Or

maybe a local farmer, who doesn't clean off the trees once the commercial harvest has been sold, would be happy to let you glean the orchard for a nominal fee. Ask vendors at the market if they, or someone else they know, might be interested in getting rid of some excess fruit.

- **Food service distributor** (like Sysco): Food service distributors deliver food to school cafeterias, restaurants, and other food establishments. They are often willing to add an order, even a small order, if they are already delivering in your area. There are numerous food service distributors all over the country. Some are small, regional companies while others are large, international corporations. Ask your local bakery or candy shop which companies they recommend.
- **Restaurant supply store or bulk food store** (like Costco): These types of stores are a good option for purchasing fruit in larger quantities than you would at the local grocery store, but smaller than a distributor or farmer may require.

At my local restaurant supply store, I can buy a 100-count bag of lemons or a 5-pound box of frozen strawberries. A food service distributor may require a minimum order of 500 lemons or a 100-pound bag of frozen fruit.

When you are starting out, purchasing smaller amounts may be more cost effective. Although five pounds of frozen strawberries costs more per pound than 100 pounds of frozen strawberries, the overall reduced expense lets you experiment with different products, without spending your whole budget. You can order fruit in greater quantities once your business is up and running.

- **Other**: Be observant. There may be other opportunities in your area to find affordable fruit supplies. Perhaps the local bakery will let you add to their blueberry order, at their price. Or a restaurant or school cafeteria will order a few things for you from their distributor. Even your local grocery store may be willing to order a couple extra cases of berries or plums, and sell them to you at a lower price. If you live in an area that grows fruit commercially, check with the packers or fruit associations. They may have excess fruit that they will practically give away if you pick it up at their convenience.

Sugar and Other Sweeteners

When making jam or other soft spreads, you need sweetener, and lots of it. Sweeteners include sugar, brown sugar, honey, and maple syrup. You will use lots of sweetener, so it's important to get the best price possible. Your ordering options are similar to the fruit options.

- **Restaurant supply store or bulk food store**: A restaurant supply store carries sugar in 25 or 50-pound bags, with a large price savings to match. I recommend purchasing these larger bags, and then transferring the sugar to smaller, food-safe plastic containers with locking lids for storage.
- **Food service distributor**: As with fruit, sometimes you can piggyback a small order with a larger food

distributor order. The order will most likely be for 25 or 50-pound bags of sugar.

- **Partner with a local business** like a bakery or candy maker: If there is a local bakery or candy maker in your area, they may be willing to add an extra bag of sugar or two to their order for you, at their price.
- **Order in bulk online**: There are several online shops where you can order bulk supplies. Usually this isn't the best option when ordering sugar, because shipping costs add up due to the heavy weight. However, if you live in an isolated or rural area, it may be less expensive than any other service, even with the added shipping cost.
- **Other**: The same options as above apply. Perhaps you could combine your order with that of the local school or daycare. The local grocery store is usually happy to order an extra case, and sell it for less than the shelf price. Do you live near a sugar plant? If so, they may be happy to sell directly if you pick up at the loading dock.

Flavorings and Other Ingredients

What additional ingredients do you need to make your soft spreads? There is nothing more frustrating than arriving at your rental kitchen space, with all your implements in tow, only to realize that you don't have all the necessary ingredients.

Don't forget to determine how much of each ingredient you need also. For example, if you make peach jam, you may use small amount of lemon juice in each batch. You will need a large bottle of lemon juice to get started, but probably don't want to order five gallons of lemon juice. The juice quality will deteriorate before you can use that much! On the other hand, those cute, little plastic lemons at the grocery store may only hold enough for 1 or 2 jam batches, leading to packaging waste and more expense than necessary.

- **Grow your own**: Do you use an ingredient that is easy to grow yourself? Perhaps your jam recipe uses fresh mint or dried borage flowers or another herb. These, and many other ingredients, can be expensive to acquire – but inexpensive to grow yourself. Do however, make sure that home-grown ingredients are allowed in your state.
- **Local farmer/farmers market**: If you don't grow your own flavorings, maybe there is a local farmer who does! Connect with them at the farmers market.
- **Restaurant supply store or bulk food store**: Restaurant supply stores and bulk food stores are a great place to find large, but not too large, containers of spices and herbs at a reasonable price.
- **Food service distributor**: Same as above. Distributors often carry flavorings, pectin, and lemon juice in larger containers than you can purchase at the grocery store.
- **Wholesale Suppliers**: Many suppliers are happy to sell you herbs or other flavorings by the pound. Although most of their business accounts are large food manufacturers, they also serve micro-businesses. I purchased herbs and spices from Oregon Spice, and other bulk flavorings from Mizkan.

- **Partner with a local business** like a bakery or candy maker: Partner with another local business and save money by splitting both the cost and the amount of additional ingredients. Your partners may even be happy to stock your completed soft spread products in their shop!
- **Order in bulk online**: Online bulk sales may be the perfect answer if you need an ingredient that is difficult to source. In past food business ventures, I purchased buttermilk powder, nutritional yeast, and lemon juice powder from an online bulk sales shop. I got a price break for ordering 5 pounds at a time. Since I only used small amounts of these ingredients, 5 pounds lasted for six months or more.

Is your business USP all-natural or wholesomeness or organic? If so, be sure to purchase cane sugar, which is made from sugar cane. Sugar made from sugar beets is less expensive, but is also made from GMO (genetically modified) ingredients. If your customers are expecting a natural product, they are probably not expecting a GMO ingredient. The sugar package will be labeled cane sugar or beet sugar. The same may be true if you use commercial pectin to thicken your spreads. Commercial pectin often contains dextrose, which may come from GMO corn.

Equipment

Soft spreads also don't require lots of fancy equipment, but you do need some supplies. Most of tools probably already have a home in your kitchen cupboard, but if not, they are readily available for a small investment.

Jars and Lids

Your soft spreads are no doubt the best tasting products in the county. But no one will ever know if you don't pique their interest. The best way to catch a customer's attention? Packaging. And soft spread packaging means jars and lids. Where will you find just the right jars at just the right price?

- **Restaurant supply stores or bulk food stores:** These stores often carry jars and lids by the case.
- **Several online companies:** Uline and Berlin Packaging, carry affordable, approved jam jars in all shapes and sizes. See Chapter 9 for more mail order sources.
- **Hardware stores:** Your local hardware store is full of all kinds of helpful equipment for canning. They are often the first stores to stock canning jars in the spring too. Most local hardware stores will be happy to place a special order or two through the year, for several cases of the jars you desire.
- **Discount stores:** Although local discount store like Dollar Stores or liquidation centers don't always have approved canning jars, sometimes they do! This is more apt to be a hit or miss source, rather than a constant source of jars and lids. However, once I purchased several cases of jars and lids at a liquidation center, for mere pennies per jar. Even if the jars are a little different from your usual jars,

they could be used for a new product or for a special event short run.

Miscellaneous Equipment

Do you have the following equipment available? Most can be purchased at the local grocery, discount, restaurant supply, or department store. Dollar stores are a small food manufacturer's best friend. Most carry a good assortment of needed equipment - for only a dollar!

- **Cooking thermometer:** The easiest way to check soft spread gel set is to check the cooking temperature. The easiest way to check the temperature is to have a thermometer! Use a standard cooking or candy thermometer that reaches at least 225 degrees Fahrenheit.
- **Long handled spoons:** For stirring cooking jam and other soft spreads
- **Measuring cups:** For measuring ingredients
- **Paper towels:** For wiping jar tops before placing lids, and for basic clean up. You can never have too many paper towels available when cooking bubbling (and spitting) jam.
- **Disposable gloves:** Use while cooking. Most states require gloves to be used while preparing any food.
- **Hairnets:** Most states also require that hairnets are used when preparing food. Even if your state does not require this, I recommend it. You NEVER want a client to find a hair in their jar of jam!
- **Notebook:** For recordkeeping. See more about how to keep track of your ingredients and product lots in the recordkeeping section in Chapter 8.

- **Food scale**: It is easier to make consistent jam batches if the ingredients are weighed instead of measured. Use a small food scale, which can be purchased for under twenty dollars.
- **Food safe storage containers**: Purchase several of these containers in various sizes. Use them to freeze fruit for later batches, or store sugar in smaller amounts in containers. This makes it easier and less physically demanding to move ingredients around while cooking.

  Be sure that your storage containers are food grade and have locking covers. Never store ingredient in garbage receptacles, even if the receptacles are brand new and clean. Garbage cans are treated with chemicals and are not food-safe.

  Food safe storage containers can be found at restaurant supply stores or mail order outlets like Berlin Packaging. Local restaurants may also have extra containers that they will either give, or sell, you. Many ingredients that restaurants purchase in bulk, like pickles, come in 5-gallon food safe plastic tubs that can be cleaned and reused. Be sure to keep all containers tightly closed. You certainly don't want your ingredients to become infected with pantry moths, house flies, fruit flies, or other pests. This could be an expensive lesson, as all infected ingredients will have to be discarded.

- **Mixing Bowls**: Just as when making jam at home, you will want an assortment of different sized bowls nearby for mixing and holding ingredients.

- **Water Bath Canner**: If working as a cottage industry, you will process jam and other soft spreads using the water bath canner method. If you are running your business from a commercial kitchen, with a state approved recipe, you may not need a canner, as the processing method may depend on temperature alone.

  Almost any large pot can be made into a water bath canner. I use a 16-quart stainless steel stock pot with a flat bottom to process jars of jam at home. It is small enough to be manageable but large enough to process two layers of jam jars at once.

  Jarden Home Brands (Ball®) has recently come out with an electric water bath canner. It is reasonably priced and has good reviews.

- **Canning rack**: If using a canner, you will need a canning rack. I am pleased with a reversible canning rack that I ordered from *Sur la Table*. It is heavier and of higher quality than most traditional basket type canner racks.

Let's Review: Time to pull your materials together!

Where will you get your needed fruit? Sugar? Other product flavorings?

Do you have all the equipment you need to make soft spreads?

What tools should you purchase? Where will you get them?

What kind of jars and lids will you use?

Do you have a notebook for record keeping?

All the miscellaneous equipment needed?

Notes

CHAPTER 7

Successful Sales Selling Your Products

"The important thing is not being afraid to take a chance. Remember, the greatest failure is to not try. Once you find something you love to do, be the best at doing it." Debbi Fields

Congratulations, your business is almost ready to launch. Jars of jewel-toned sweet spreads await eager customers, leading us to the most exciting step – actually making some money! Where will you sell your jams? What will your jam offering be? And most importantly – what will you charge?

How to Determine Price

Figuring how much to charge requires a little bit of math. Don't worry – this is the kind of math you use every day when deciding whether or not to purchase a new car, if those cute boots are worth the expense, and how to divide the restaurant dinner bill among friends.

There are several ways to determine the price of your jams, but let's usc thc casiest approach.

Step 1: Ingredient Costs

Determine how much you pay for each ingredient in the recipe. Let's use our peach butter recipe.

18-20 medium peaches (about 6 pounds)
4 cups granulated sugar
8 (half-pint) jars

For this example, let's say you purchased a 25-pound box of peaches from the local farmer for $20. Thus, one pound of peaches cost 80 cents ($20 divided by 25 pounds) and six pounds cost $2.40 (.80 multiplied by six). So, the peaches needed for this batch cost us $2.40, since we need 6 pounds of peaches.

Four cups of sugar equals about 2 pounds. We know this because we weighed the sugar using our small food scale (see, I told you it would be useful). You purchased sugar at the grocery store and paid $4 for a four-pound bag. Therefore, the sugar for this batch cost you $2.00, or $1 per pound. (Sugar purchased from a restaurant supply store in 25-pound bags will be even less).

Of course, making jam requires jars! Each empty jar costs you about .75 or $6 total for the batch of eight.

Perhaps the labels cost another .25 each, or an additional $2 for this particular batch (8 x .25, or one label for each jar).

The grand total is $12.40 for the batch, or $1.55 per jar ($12.40 divided by 8). If you work from home this is basically your cost per jar of soft spread. Let's check our work:

$$\frac{\$20}{25} \textit{pounds of peaches} = \$.80 \textit{ per pound of peaches}$$

$$\$.80x6 \textit{ pounds peaches} = \$2.40 \textit{ for the peaches per batch}$$

$$4 \textit{ pounds sugar cost } \$4 \textit{ thus } 1 \textit{ pound of sugar cost } \$1$$

$$4 \textit{ cups of sugar} = 2 \textit{ pounds thus } \$1\ x\ 2 = \$2, \textit{total cost of sugar.}$$

$$\$.75 \textit{ per jar } x\ 8 \textit{ jars} = \$6 \textit{ total}$$

$$\$.25 \textit{ per label } x\ 8 \textit{ jars} = \$2 \text{ total}$$

$$\textit{Total batch} = \$12.40\ (2.40 + 2.0 + 6 + 2)$$

$$\textit{Each jar} = \$1.55\ (12.40 \textit{ divided by } 8)$$

However, if you rent commercial space you will have to take the rental costs into account also, including the actual rental time and the car mileage (currently 57.5 cents per mile, 2020) used to get to the rental location. So, if the rental costs you $20/hour, and you make twenty jars in that hour, each jar costs you another $1. Of course, this shows immediately that it would be more cost effective to work for 4-5 hours instead of just one hour (so you only have to set up and tear down once). Perhaps you can make 20 jars in one hour, but 150 jars in 5 hours. If so, despite the extra rental expense, your cost reduces to 50 cents per jar due to your increased efficiency.

Step 2: Wholesale Price

There are many ways to determine wholesale price, but a good rule of thumb is to double your cost ($1.55 x 2) to set the wholesale price, thus $3.10 per jar.

Step 3: Retail Price

Double the wholesale price to set a suggested retail price, or $6.20 per jar retail ($3.10 x 2).

Step 4: Cost Effectiveness

Do a market comparison. Is $6.20 per jar a reasonable price? How are other similar products priced? Don't compare yourself to grocery store jams unless you are planning to start a huge business. This is where your USP, identified in Chapter 1, becomes important. You don't want to compete on price! Looking at other artisan jams and butters, $6 per jar is a reasonable price. There are several other methods to determine wholesale and retail prices, but the above method is the easiest to use, especially when just getting your business off the ground.

Step 5: Efficiencies

Once you set your price, search for ways to decrease your costs and increase your profit margin without reducing your product quality. For example, maybe the local farmer will sell you 50 pounds of peaches for $30 instead of the usual $40. Perhaps you can purchase sugar from a restaurant supply store or get the local baker to order from his supplier for you. Research different jars that can be purchased for even less.

Don't be tempted to reduce your price. Remember, just because you can purchase peaches inexpensively today, doesn't mean that they will still be available at that price next month. You need to give yourself a little wiggle room so that you aren't repricing products every month.

> *Ingredient prices have a tendency to increase when you least expect. During the first four years we manufactured soup mixes, our main ingredient quadrupled in price. While we did raise our product prices a bit, most of our increased costs were offset by production efficiencies and less expensive packaging.*

How much do your products cost to create? Following the above steps, work through the equations for each of your tentative soft spreads. It's ok to use grocery store ingredient prices for this initial costing exercise. It gives you some idea of just how much your profit margin might be.

Is the Recipe Cost Effective?

What if your product isn't cost effective? How depressing. You are excited to get started. You are emotionally invested in your new jam business baby. Then, like bucket of cold water, you find that none of your jam ideas can pay for themselves. Or that one or two of your products are too expensive to produce. Or that the jars you have your heart set on cost way too much. Don't despair, all may not be lost. There are several ways to reduce costs.

- **Go back to Step 5 above**: Research less expensive ways to acquire your fruit or main ingredient.
- **Buy in larger bulk sizes**: Take a chance and purchase 500 pounds of sugar instead of 50 pounds. The cost per unit will be much less. Do remember that you need to have an approved location to store the sugar. Your garage probably won't meet food safety guidelines.
- **Clearance Sales**: Watch for end-of-season clearance sales or liquidation sales. Some physical or online stores may offer their extra jars at a discounted rate after the summer season is over. This is the time to stock up.
- **Recipe Makeover**: Change your recipe or the products you offer. If the recipe uses a high cost ingredient, figure out if you can substitute a less expensive, but similar, ingredient.
- **Moving On**: If the cost is still too high, set the product idea aside and move on to a different product. This can be difficult, especially if you are emotionally attached to your special *saffron apple jam* or *prickly pear jelly*.

Unless you grow acres of your own crocus, the cost of saffron will most likely push your jam price too high. And if you live in Minnesota, you probably won't have a steady, inexpensive supply of prickly pear fruit. This situation is a good time to remember why you are starting a soft spreads business – to make money! Stick to making a small batch of saffron apple jam for your family each year, and pivot your product offering to cinnamon apple jam or star anise apple jam. Still good options. Still unique and creative. Even better; affordable.

Selling Retail or Wholesale

Will you sell your beautiful jams wholesale, or retail, or both?

Wholesale

Wholesale means selling goods in large quantities at a lower rate, like the wholesale price you determined above. Your wholesale accounts will be established stores. The stores then sell your scrumptious jams to customers at a retail price. For example, you may sell a case of your soft spreads to your local specialty foods store, Karen's Gourmet Foods. Karen purchases your items at the wholesale cost you set, or $3.10 per jar in our above example. She may sell your products at the retail price you set, $6.20, or she may sell it for different price, maybe $5.90 or $6.50 per jar.

Wholesale Advantages

There are many advantages to selling wholesale. For example, wholesale means you sell in bulk, usually one or more cases at a time instead of one jar at a time. This saves you time since someone else worries about stocking shelves and selling each jar. You also can wait and manufacture your jams once you receive an order, thus only making as much as you know you can sell.

Wholesale Disadvantages

But there are also disadvantages when selling wholesale. Your profit is less per jar than if you were selling retail. You may need to hire a sales representative to reach a larger distribution area, resulting in another cost eating into your profit, since most sales representatives expect to be paid! You will have to devise a shipping strategy and policy, and will spend time packing your product for shipping.

Often, prospective wholesale buyers request free product samples before deciding to add them to their shelves. These samples, and the associated shipping expenses, will be unredeemed costs. Also, if you operate your business as a cottage industry, many states ONLY allow retail sales, not wholesale sales.

Retail

Retail means selling directly to the end consumer. For example, selling one or two jars to your neighbor Bob, or selling to customers at a farmer's market or a craft show.

Here you will charge your retail price, which is $6.20 per jar in the above example.

Retail Advantages

There is one primary advantage to selling your jams and soft spreads on a retail basis; all profits are yours. You do not share the income with a sales representative or store owner. You also have closer contact with the consumer. Chatting with or observing customers helps you determine which products are popular and which are less so.

Retail Disadvantages

But there are trade-offs when selling retail. Retail sales or direct sales take up much more of your time. To make money you will regularly be attending craft shows or farmer's markets. You will be responsible for setting up and breaking down your display area. You will spend more time selling soft spreads, and less time actually producing soft spreads. Whether you consider this an advantage or a disadvantage depends on how much help you have, and which part of the business you enjoy most. While you may have started your business to make jam, it's just a hobby until you start selling jam! The business requires both tasks.

Consignment

Maybe you can harness the best of both worlds and sell some of your product via consignment. Consignment sales usually fall somewhere in between wholesale and retail sales. You may receive 85% of the retail sales price for every jar sold, and the shop owner receives 15%, or a similar break.

Consignment Advantages

Much like selling wholesale, the advantage of selling by consignment is that someone else is responsible for the actual selling of your product, thus you don't have to be present to sell.

Consignment Disadvantages

But the disadvantage is that you don't get paid until a customer takes your product from the shelf and purchases it. Some consignment shops don't keep very good records, thus you may not get paid even if the product is sold, unless you check the store frequently.

Where Will You Sell Your Products?

At first glance, there seems to only be a few places to sell your jams and other soft spreads. But now is the time to think creatively! In fact, I would argue that small soft spread manufacturers have greater opportunities, in more sites, than do large manufacturers. No, you probably won't sell cases and cases of your jams at the local Walmart®, Costco®, or Kroger®. But the large manufacturers are not going to be found on the shelves at your local specialty foods store, and your label is just what these types of stores, and their customers, are seeking.

Luckily jams and other sweet spreads are highly desired products and there are several places where you can sell them. How many of these options might work for you?

Farmer's Markets

A farmer's market is a group of produce and related vendors, located in one location, usually for 2-6 hours a day, one or two days a week – although some markets are open daily and/or year-round.

Markets may be operated by a non-profit organization, the local municipal government, or a volunteer group. Farmer's markets are usually thrilled to have local food manufacturers participate, especially in the spring and late fall when there are fewer fresh produce vendors. Your jams will help draw people to the market, plus you will get immediate feedback from customers about what they like and don't like – helping you determine which products to keep, which to abandon, and which to put on hiatus. Farmer's markets are retail markets for you. Some farmers' markets require that you pay an annual fee for your space, while others charge a percentage of your total sales.

Farm Stands

A farm stand is usually operated by one person or entity. Some are year-round, others are simply a table put at the end of the drive whenever a farmer has product to sell. If you already have a farm stand for your own farm or garden produce, it makes sense to add your jam to the mix. If not, perhaps a local farm stand owner would be willing to sell your jams. Some purchase products wholesale, but smaller stands may be willing to try consignment sales. Do keep good records, so you know how many jars of each type of jam you left at the stand. And check back often to restock.

Local Craft Shows

Local craft shows can be both great fun and lucrative. – if you choose the right show. Artisan soft spreads usually don't sell well at vendor fairs, which are shows that offer mass produced items like Mary Kay Cosmetics or LuLaRoe clothing.

But if you participate in a craft show that specializes in home crafted products, you may do very well. These customers are looking for something special and expect to pay more for high quality items.

Three things to consider before participating in a craft show:

- **Early sign up**: The slate of vendors is often filled months before the actual show. So, if you want to participate in a Christmas show, plan to submit your application in June.
- **Entry fee**: Also, the entry fee can be quite expensive, anywhere from $300 to $2400 or more, whereas a vendor fair may only have a $20 entry fee. Make sure you have enough product inventory to cover your costs.
- **Booth display**: Participating in a craft show means that you will have to design your booth, set it up, and tear it down. You, or someone who helps you, will have to man the booth during the whole show, whether it is a one day show or a one-week

commitment. Working a craft show requires a bit of stamina and physical strength.

Craft shows are retail markets thus, you do reap the entire purchase price for every jar of jam you sell. Some small jam businesses only operate over the holiday season, selling enough product at three or four selective shows to reach their annual financial goals.

If you provide tasting samples (and you should), some states require a temporary health department license. The license must be from the local health department, in the area of the show. For example, if you manufacture your products in Smith County, but the show is in Jones County, the license should be issued in Jones County. Craft show organizers will no doubt be able to help you meet all local requirements.

Local Food Events

Is there a local food event in your area? Food events are like craft shows, although every booth offers a different kind of locally produced food instead of a variety of handicrafts. Entrants may include caterers, food trucks, restaurants, bakers, candy makers, and other specialty food makers. This would be a retail market for you. If there isn't one of these events locally, perhaps you could start one!

Local Grocery Stores

Sometimes local grocery stores save a bit of shelf space for locally produced products. This is especially true of independent grocers or small chain stores. Your jam probably won't be displayed next to the store brand jams, but will be with the higher priced artisan and natural food products – just where you want it. Pitch the store manager with your products and ask what your next steps may be. Keep in mind this would be a wholesale market for you, not a retail market.

Local Gift Shops

Gift shops love locally produced specialty foods, especially items like jams, whose jewel-toned jars show so well on the shelf. While this is a wholesale market, if you are willing to sell partial or mixed cases of items, and re-stock often, gift shops may become your best customer. We established wonderful partnerships with two gift shops; one local and another several hours away. Because we were responsive when they needed half-cases, we ended up selling them hundreds of cases each year.

Local Specialty Stores

Specialty stores like butcher shops and farm supply stores are surprisingly good outlets for your products. What does jam have to do with a butcher shop? Probably nothing, except that customers for both expect quality. Therefore, the local butcher shop may love to display a few jars of your jam. They will be even more interested if you offer free recipes cards using your jam with some of their products; like a Blackberry Jam Glazed Pork Chop Recipe, or Slow Cooked Beef Stew with Orange Marmalade. This would be another wholesale market that may request small or mixed case lots. They also may be open to consignment sales.

Local Restaurants

Chain restaurants probably won't be willing to stock your soft spreads, but local restaurants may be thrilled to both purchase your jams wholesale for their breakfast table, and offer jars retail to prospective buyers. On a recent trip, our breakfast came with a pot of beautiful, homemade strawberry jam. The server noted that if we liked it, we could purchase some in the gift shop. Again, this option is most likely if you are willing to split cases, offer smaller cases, or offer to sell via consignment.

Your Website

Have you ever broken your ankle? While it's possible to hobble around with a heavy cast, using crutches makes the whole process easier. It's the same with a business. While it's possible to operate without a website, having one provides appreciated support. Today it's easier than ever to sell product via your own site. Set up a sales page on your site, and connect with PayPal® for payment. Orders will come to your email address. One advantage of this sales method is that instead of paying a monthly charge for an ecommerce page, PayPal® only charges you a fee for each order. Also, in these days of hacking, the PayPal® site is much more secure, therefore you won't have to worry too much about having a customer credit card number breach. Anyone can pay via PayPal®, even if they don't have a PayPal® account.

It's also a good idea to collect visitor email addresses using a sign-up form. Customers who complete the form are already interested in your products! Adding them to a mailing list lets you send occasional emails promoting your new jams and jellies, or special sales, or events that you are participating in. A mailing list is also a wonderful way to keep in touch with your customers, and helps build a relationship.

Etsy, Inc.

If setting up a business website store in the beginning is overwhelming, you could set up your own Etsy shop. Etsy has many of the same advantages as PayPal®. You never see or collect customer credit card numbers, and Etsy takes care of payment security. It costs a bit more to sell via Etsy than your own site, but is still very affordable. You will set up an Etsy store, pay a small fee for each listed product, and another small fee when you sell product. However, you won't have to set up a storefront from scratch. Every Etsy store looks the same, and it is simple to design your own store.

Amazon.com, Inc.

You may be able to sell jams and other soft spreads through an Amazon.com seller program. Selling food products on Amazon requires following their Pro Plan, which at this writing is $39.99 a month, plus additional fees. Be prepared to submit copies of your licenses and other information before acceptance into the program.

State Specific Catalogs and Stores

Does your state have a craft or artisan-based state outlet like Made in Washington, or Made in Oregon, or Maine Made? These fantastic programs don't accept every product, but don't give up if your soft spreads get turned down the first year. These agencies usually like to see some years of experience before including your products in their catalogs or stores. Nonetheless, submit your products for their consideration today. You never know, it may be just the item they are seeking.

Church or School Bazaars

Bazaars can be great options when you are testing the waters or only have a small amount of product to sell. Some bazaars are tiny, with few vendors and customers. These can still be helpful because you will have immediate feedback from the purchasers. Other bazaars are large and lucrative. For example, there is a bazaar in my area that often has a several years-long waiting list. The bazaar is always the first Saturday in December, one day only, and is held as a school fundraiser. It has the reputation as a great place to find unusual Christmas gifts, draws a large crowd, and many vendors sell thousands of dollars of product every year.

Hobby Groups

Offer a holiday special to your book group or your quilt group. While most of your friends and acquaintances have no interest in constantly receiving a sales pitch, they may love an annual *friends sale*. You could run a 2-week special over the holidays, or a business anniversary sale, or similar event, specifically for your social groups. Hand out printed flyers at your next book club meeting, or post a notice to your Facebook groups.

Social Media

Social media can be the best way to expeditiously reach several potential customers. Periodically remind your friends and followers about your jams. This is best done of course if you have a business Facebook page or Twitter, Instagram, or Pinterest account. But you can still remind your personal friends about your sales page, especially when coupled with a special offer.

Trade Shows

Trade shows are like craft shows for the wholesale market. Only pre-approved buyers are allowed to attend, and the shows are not open to the public. Participating in trade shows is quite expensive, however, the exposure may bring in orders for cases and cases of jams. Most producers do not expect to break even when attending a trade show. They expect the show to provide long term exposure that they otherwise would not receive. Trade shows are usually held in larger cities.

Enlist Professional Help

Maybe it's time to enlist the help of a sales representative. Think of a sales representative as a modern-day tinker, carrying his wares from town to town. Except instead of sewing needles and squeeze mops, the wares he carries are your jams, jellies, and soft spreads.

A specialty foods sales representative offers retail buyers a variety of products made by small manufacturers just like you. They usually cover a specific geographic area, and two or three times each year visit specialty foods shops, farm stands, wineries, and more to offer products for sale. They take orders from these retail establishments, and then you fill and ship the orders to that location. You pay the sales representative a percentage, usually 10-20% of the order wholesale price.

> *How do you determine if a particular sales representative is right for you and for your business? Don't be tempted to work with the first sales representative who agrees to sell your products. You want the rep to be a good fit. Our first representative established several accounts for us, but never really understood our product. As a result, many of those accounts were short-term, only placing an order once or twice. Work with a sales representative who understands how your products are unique, and is enthusiastic about representing them.*

Using a sales representative can be a blessing, especially if you don't particularly like selling. Although the sales rep makes the first contact with the customer, the stores may call you directly to re-order. If so, that's great, it's always a good idea to have a relationship with your customers. But if the account was established by the sales representative, you still need to pay their 10-20% on the reorder. This is only fair, as the sales representative made the initial contact, sold your product to the store, established the account, and will check in with them the next time they are in that area. Ask your local specialty food establishments if they have a favorite sales representative they recommend for your products.

Other Options

Don't limit potential sales opportunities. If you are willing to sell small amounts of jars or sell via consignment, you may be able to sell as many jars as you want every year. Consider less obvious outlets like hotel gift shops, hospital gift shops, school fundraisers, local museums, kitchen shops, and cooking schools.

Keep an open mind and don't automatically discount a location unless it does not meet your USP. For example, if your USP is Local, you probably won't want to sell at the Import Shop, or if your USP is Artisan, don't plan to sell at the big box store. Do avoid any locations that will expect your product to be inexpensive. We don't want our artisan, specialty products competing based on price.

You are getting closer! Review, using the following Notes page.

How much does product A cost you?

How much does product B cost you?

How much does product C cost you?

Are your recipes cost effective? If not, what changes can you make so that the cost per piece is reasonable?

Where will you sell your products? Do you want to sell wholesale? Retail? Both?

Will you open an Etsy store or your own website store?

Jot down some local establishments or craft shows that might be a good fit for your jams.

Go to **ReneePottle.com/Profitable-Preserves** to receive a PDF copy of this checklist.

Notes

CHAPTER 8

A Shrewd Eye
Managing Your Business

"I love money. I love everything about it. I bought some pretty good stuff. Got me a $300 pair of socks. Got a fur sink. An electric dog polisher. A gasoline powered turtleneck sweater. And, of course, I bought some dumb stuff too." Steve Martin

You are a success! You are known locally as the jam lady or jam guy. Now it's time to ensure that you are managing your business so it meets all your needs. Maybe you want to grow your business, or just make it the best business it can be. Here are some things to keep in mind as you refine or expand:

Managing a Successful Business

No matter how large or small, all businesses require some basic management functions. Stay current on these tasks and you won't find yourself in crisis mode when faced with an unexpected event.

Taxes

While your business is young, you may not sell enough to pay quarterly taxes, only annual taxes. However, as your business grows, if you expect to owe the IRS more than $1000 at the end of the year, you must switch and pay taxes quarterly. Individual states may also require quarterly taxes.

Employees

One can only make so much jam alone before needing assistance. Do you have a family member who would like to help out in the kitchen? Or do you need an occasional or part-time hire? The rules differ for each.

- **Teens**: Young teens, 14-15 years old, are not allowed to cook, although you can have your teen wash and prepare fruit, pack the finished product for shipping, and wash and clean your cooking equipment. Older teens can help with cooking as long as there is no open flame.
- **Occasional Employees**: You can hire occasional employees or contract employees. The IRS considers each category differently, depending on hours worked, salary earned, attendance requirements, and more. Consult with your tax accountant or attorney to determine which category your employee meets.

- **Part-time Workers**: Part-time employees must meet all state and federal guidelines. Be prepared to pay payroll taxes, and keep good records.

Keep in mind that all business with employees must have a federal EIN number. See Chapter 5 for more information about the EIN number and Chapter 9 for helpful EIN resources.

Policies

You will need policies sooner rather than later, especially if you hire employees or sell via wholesale. You should have policies related to payments, shipping, damaged goods, and human resource policies if you have employees.
If the thought of writing policies makes you weep with despair, cheer up! I am not talking about long, boring, undecipherable documents full of legalese.

The joy of a small business is that your policies can be small too – often just one sentence, especially if you don't have employees. For example, a shipping policy might be, *Orders shipped via Fedex from Wherearewe, USA*. See Chapter 9 for a simple *Wholesale Bulletin* – a document that rolls all your shipping, payment, and ordering information into one or two pages.

Business Plan

Do you need a business plan? Or do you need a plan for your business? If you are seeking outside funding due to business growth, then it's time to write a formal business plan. You will find several resources in Chapter 9 to help you write your own plan. A formal business plan is required by almost any bank, venture capitalist, the Small Business Administration, or any other commercial funder. A formal business plan includes financial information and projections, sales information, competitor analysis, product descriptions, and company information.

If you are not seeking funds, you probably won't need a formal business plan. Everyone should have a plan for their business though. Now that you have operated your business for a while, it's time to formalize your growth projections, determine how much space you need and when you will need it, consider if you will need employees and how to pay for them, determine where to get increased amounts of ingredients, identify additional markets, and so on. This can be done on one piece of paper or in a large document. Whatever works for you. The difference is that a *formal business plan* is a document for you and for outside investors. A *plan for your business* is a guidance document just for you.

Equipment

If you've ever tried to double or triple a batch of jam, you know how quickly it can become a sticky, scorched mess. So, once your orders have grown, you may want to invest in specialized equipment that lets you make more than eight jars of jam per batch.

Making and selling large amounts of jams every week can quickly become overwhelming. Since we cannot double or triple soft spread batches (except fruit butters), making two batches of peach jam each week may be delightful – and you will be excited to sell so much product. Making 20 batches each week is probably going to become tiresome, even though you are still delighted to sell so much jam. Special commercial equipment like a Cooker/Evaporator and a Jam Filling Unit lets you to make large batches of jam without affecting quality.

Space

If you start your business in your kitchen, it may quickly seem that the room shrinks and you have outgrown it. Now is the perfect time to look for commercial kitchen rental space, or to invest in building a commercial kitchen in the garage.

Remember, you can probably find commercial kitchen rental space at your local food incubator, or at local bakeries, restaurants, Grange halls, private schools, wineries, breweries, or other small food manufacturers. Direct competitors probably won't rent you kitchen space, but small specialty producers like mustard or granola manufacturers may be thrilled to rent you space during their down time. Make a list of potential options in your area, and then contact each.

Hiring Professionals

As your business grows, so does your need for professional advice. If you did not use a Certified Public Accountant (CPA) or a lawyer when establishing your business, now is the time to seek their advice. A CPA in particular can help you with the financial matters that most of us avoid, like state and federal taxes, payroll taxes, and bookkeeping services.

Other professionals: web designer, virtual assistant, copywriter, and graphic designer, can all be helpful when expanding your jam business too.

- **Web Designer**: A web designer will upgrade and update your web site, introducing you to new markets and increasing product sales.
- **Virtual Assistant**: A virtual assistant can post invoices, chase payments, manage orders, issue press releases, and numerous other administrative tasks.
- **Copywriter**: Copywriters are the wordsmiths who write your tantalizing product labels, catalogs, and point-of-sale marketing materials.
- **Designers**: Graphic Designers often work in tandem with the copywriter, designing eye-catching labels and marketing materials.

Your Health

There is nothing more exciting and rewarding than planning, starting, and managing your own business. It's almost like bringing a new child into being, and can be just as physically draining. While making soft spreads does not require the help of an obstetrician, there is still a fair amount of labor involved. Standing and stirring jam till it gels, packing and moving boxes of finished jars for shipping, and wrangling 50 or 100-pound bags of sugar, all can take a toll on the body if you try to do too much yourself.

All of these tasks may be a great way to get in shape and make money at the same time – and it beats paying for gym time – but don't overestimate your own stamina. Hire help when needed, and use mobility aids like hand trucks to lighten the load.

Record Keeping

No matter how big or small your business, good record keeping is a must. Start capturing appropriate information using a small notebook, 3-ring binder, or digital table/spreadsheet.

Production Records

Every time you make a new batch of jam, keep track of the ingredient and process details. Note:

- Date the soft spread batch was prepared
- Daily batch number; i.e. first batch of the day
- Number of jars made per batch
- How each batch was processed/prepared
- Processing time for each batch
- Ingredients included in each batch
- Where the ingredients were purchased
- Ingredient lot numbers if available
- Who prepared each particular batch of jam
- Identifying product batch/lot number

For example, your peaches may have come from the neighborhood farmer, the sugar may be Domino Brand lot # 12345, and the lemon juice may be ReaLemon® #ffggh.

Production Record: Peach Butter

Date	Daily Batch #	# Jars	Processing	Processing Time	Ingredients	Where Sourced	Lot #	Preparer	Product Batch or Lot #
8/14/20	1	8	Water bath	15 min	Peaches Sugar/Domino	Smith Farm Joe's Restaurant Supply	None 12345	Renee	011
8/14/20	2	8	Same as above	Same above	Same above	Same above	Same above	Same above	002
8/16/20	1	10	Water bath	15 min	Peaches Sugar/C & H	Smith Farm Joe's Restaurant Supply	None Ab105	Renee	003

Documenting this information will help you track your products if a problem arises down the road. For example, while rare, one of your ingredients may be recalled. If so, you want to know which of your jam lots contain this ingredient so you can pull it from inventory.

Look at almost any shelf stable food and you will find a lot number. Be sure to give each batch of product you make a lot# too. No agency tells you what lot number to use, you decide what works best for you. In the above example I used a triple lot number, 001, 002, and so on. Lot number stickers don't have to be fancy at all. You can place a simple, handwritten sticker on the bottom of each jar. You may want to also include a best-by date on the same sticker too.

Use the easiest record keeping method for you; perhaps trying two or three different methods in the beginning. For example, I personally found it easier to keep track of product lot numbers by using an old-fashioned 3-ring binder. Each time I made a new batch, I wrote down all the pertinent information in the notebook. Of course, I could have done the same thing using my laptop computer, but I didn't want to get the laptop sticky. Since I am a rather messy cook, this was a real concern for me, but you are no doubt neater.

Product Sales and Inventory Record:

If you are keeping track of how many jars of jam you make, you will also want to keep track of how many jars of jam you sell!

Again, this doesn't have to be a fancy, involved spreadsheet. It can be a simple hand-drawn table if you want. I used something similar to the figure below. A table like this helps you quickly see who orders the most of each of your products. It also lets you know at a glance, whether it's time to prepare a new batch of Peach Butter, or how long it takes to sell all your Peach Syrup.

Sales and Inventory Record: Peach Butter

Date	# Jars on hand/Inventory	Account	Wholesale or Retail	# Jars sold	Contact Person
8/14/20	100				
8/14/20		Bob Smith's Farm Stand	Wholesale	24	Bob Smith
8/16/20	86				
8/21/20		Country Craft Show	Retail	61	Country Craft Shows, Inc.
8/22/20	25				

Business Expenses

There are many advantages of owning a business, even a micro-business. Your jam and jelly business may provide you with extra cash for life's little luxuries. It may help you turn excess garden produce into a usable product and appeal to your sense of sustainability. It may provide you with a growing sense of purpose and pride. But it also can reduce your taxes! Many expenses you incur, like advertising, travel, and supplies, can be deducted on your income tax return. Other property, like buildings and expensive equipment, can be depreciated on your income tax return. These deductions reduce your taxable-income, thus you pay less in taxes than you would otherwise.

Business Income

Naturally, you will keep track of your business income also. After all, income is the reason you are in business! Keep track of wholesale sales as they happen, and retail sales daily. There are many ways to do this; jot them down in a notebook, fill out old-fashioned receipt books (where you give one copy to the customer and the carbon copy stays in the book), online programs you can access with your smart phone in real time, or any other system that makes sense to you. Do not wait until January, and then try to re-create all of your sales while preparing for tax season. This non-method of record keeping induces stress and results in either over-estimating or under-estimating actual sales.

Business Documentation

Don't be overwhelmed by record keeping. It will be fairly simple, especially in the start-up phase, as you won't have exorbitant amounts of expenses or sales. Do keep either paper or digital copies of the following:

- Sales receipts; both for things you buy and products you sell
- Bank deposit receipts
- Invoices
- Credit card receipts/statements

Simple is best. Yes, you can learn lots of new software or follow some expert's new bookkeeping method. However, the system that has always worked best for me, and may work for you also, is to place each month's receipts in a manilla envelope labeled with the current month and year. At the end of the month, transfer the information to your paper or online sales and expense sheets.

Bookkeeping Aids

Do you do your own personal taxes? If so, completing your business taxes won't be much of a challenge. However, if your eyes glaze over at the word taxes, you may want to hire an accountant. In the meantime, there are several software programs that are helpful and will keep your business records in a professional manner. QuickBooks® has long been the premier small business accounting software, and is fairly easy to use. If your business is so small that small business software is still too elaborate, use the personal version of QuickBooks®, Quicken®. Other similar accounting programs include FreshBooks® and Xero™.

If old-fashioned paper records make more sense to you, keep track of all of your expenses and sales using a data entry journal of some sort. You can even design your own by making a series of tables. Draw lines on a sheet of paper like we used to in elementary school. Make sure you have columns for the date, the expense or the sale, and the amount. Even this simple step will save you money when hiring an accountant or bookkeeper.

Growing – or Not

Do you want your little jam business to grow into a mid-size organization with 100 employees? Or do you dream of it becoming a major player in the soft spread world, with jars of your favorite spread found in every grocery store in the country? Good for you. If this is your goal, keep in mind that your role will necessarily change as your business grows.

Employees

Maybe you are the most energetic man or woman on the planet, but you still need to sleep. Therefore, you cannot operate a medium or large size business by yourself. You need employees to help: make the products, ship the orders, find new markets, keep a constant flow of ingredients, keep an adequate inventory, identify and test new product offerings, pay the bills and payroll, pay licenses and taxes, prepare budgets and strategic plans, etc. Yes, you will do all of the above yourself when just starting out. Taking care of everything yourself is more manageable when you are selling 150 jars of jam a month, less so when you are selling 1500 or 15,000 jars each month. As the business grows, your role will naturally move from being the *maker* to the *manager*.

Debt

At some point a growing business needs an influx of cash to jump to the next level. This is the time to write a proper business plan and seek funding. Leaping from a small business to a mid-sized business means purchasing and storing larger amounts of ingredients than ever before. It may involve new equipment, nutrition testing and labeling, and hiring food representatives, brokers, and distributors. This step will almost always involve taking on debt. How much debt are you comfortable holding? If your dream is to be in every grocery store in the United States, and your product demand is exploding, then you will no doubt be happy to take on debt and make it work for you. However, if you are uncomfortable owing others thousands of dollars, it may be time to re-consider your business growth.

> *The business was going well. Our products were in over 100 stores in six states. After squeaking through the Great Recession, orders were increasing again. Ingredient prices were stable, and packaging prices were still affordable. But we were running out of space at the rental kitchen. And it was more difficult to find a large chunk of available kitchen cooking time. Plus, there was just too much work for one person; even with occasional family assistance. I could no longer prepare the product, deliver and ship orders, and keep the records myself. Something had to happen. Continuing meant hiring help and finding, or building, new kitchen space. Which meant getting a business loan of some sort. What to do?*

Embrace Serendipity

I once knew an enthusiastic entrepreneur, who was just starting her soft spreads company. She studied processes, bought expensive specialty equipment, and even imported unique jam jars from Europe. Her products were interesting and flavorful. Sales increased and she hired a part-time kitchen employee and a sales representative. Soon she was selling jams and fruit butters all over the region.

But then the economy hit the Great Recession. Soft spread sales slowed. Approaching the situation creatively, she started making a few jam tarts to sell at the farmer's market – mostly to showcase her soft spreads. Soon she was selling more tarts every week than jars of jam.

So, she embraced serendipity and changed her whole business approach. No more wholesale jam sales. No fancy jars or sales reps. She made enough jam for the tarts, and for many years happily sold jam tarts at local events.

Your original jam business idea may change too. The economy may slow. Ingredients may become scarce due to drought or an untimely frost. Or your business may expand your horizons and introduce you to new customer needs. This happened to Tabitha Stroup of *Friend in Cheeses Jam Company*. Tabitha realized that local farmers had extra, unsold fruit following harvest. One thing led to another and she soon started a related business, *Terroir in a Jar*. *Terroir in a Jar* operates like a co-packer, turning that excess fruit into value-added products like jams, syrups, and vinegars. The finished product then goes back to the farmers to sell at their farm stands or markets.

Friend in Cheeses Jams remains a successful company, making and selling unique jams and other soft spreads. But by embracing serendipity, Tabitha expanded the business into an additional related endeavor.

Staying Small

We grow up thinking that bigger is better. That success means having our product in every retail establishment in the country. It just seems natural to work harder and keep growing our business.

But maybe you are happy with a small, one-person business that you operate in your spare time. That's great. Don't let others define your success and push you into growing your business into something you don't want. Remember why you started this business. Maybe your goal has been to make enough money to go on a vacation, or pay for new living room furniture, or to cover Christmas presents. If you enjoy your small, one-person, solo business, then that's the way it should stay.

In my own business, I had three choices:

- I could stop seeking new markets and stay at the current size.
- I could go for it, and continue growing the business.
- I could sell the business.

It was a business that I loved, but after seven years I was tired. I didn't want to take on debt. I didn't want to manage employees. And I didn't want to build my own certified kitchen space. Initially, I scaled back, reducing product variety and selling only wholesale, not retail. After a year, I sold the business to enthusiastic new owners.

Success doesn't necessarily mean bigger. It doesn't mean rigidly sticking to one idea. Success means achieving your goals. Small can be beautiful. Flexible can be brilliant. After all, it's YOUR business. Make sure it works for YOU.

Now let's pull our plans together!

Do you need employees to get your jam business started?

Do you perhaps have some family members who can help out?

Have you developed needed policies? Designed a simple Wholesale Bulletin?

Do you need a formal business plan? Or a simple plan for your business?

Are you planning to enlist the help of a CPA? A web designer? A virtual assistant?

Have you decided how you will keep your records? Will you use a notebook? Or use a digital program?

Do you need some home bookkeeping software? Which program will you use?

Have you chosen your business launch date? Write it down. Congratulations, you are a new business owner!

Go to **ReneePottle.com/Profitable-Preserves** to receive a PDF copy of this checklist.

Notes

CHAPTER 9

Reliable Resources Helpful Information for Business Success

"All our dreams can come true, if we have the courage to pursue them." Walt Disney

Business Start-up and Completion Checklist

✓	Date	NA	
			I identified 3 potential soft spread products.
			My product recipes meet state and local guidelines.
			I have chosen a business USP.
			My food preservation skills are up-to-date.

			I have chosen: cottage industry, or small manufacturer, or building my own commercial kitchen. (Identify which)
			I have decided between: long-cooking or quick-cooking products. (ID which)
			I chose a great name for my business.
			I decided on a legal business entity: sole proprietor, partnership, LLC, or S-corp. (ID)
			I obtained my local business license.
			I obtained my state reseller's license.
			I obtained my state Department of Agriculture license/approval.
			I obtained my local Health Department approval.
			I obtained my EIN number.
			I obtained my food handler's card.
			I opened a business checking account.
			I obtained a business credit card or a credit card for my business.
			I set up a PayPal® or Google Wallet account.
			I set up a Square account.
			I am pursuing a bank merchant account.
			I obtained business insurance.
			My product front labels are designed and printed.
			My product back labels are designed and printed.
			I joined GS1 for UPC labels.
			I found a source for fruit for my

			products.
			I found a source for sugar/sweeteners for my product.
			I found a source for other needed ingredients.
			I found a source for jars and lids.
			I purchased needed miscellaneous equipment.
			I got a record keeping notebook (physical or digital).
			I determined my wholesale and retail prices for each product.
			I did a market price comparison.
			I determined that my products are cost effective.
			I decided to sell wholesale.
			I decided to sell retail.
			I decided to sell via consignment.
			I identified several potential markets.
			I have a website for my business.
			I opened an Etsy store for my business.
			I set up business social media accounts.
			I developed a payment policy.
			I developed a shipping policy.
			I wrote a simple plan for my business.
			I wrote a formal business plan.
			I enlisted the help of a graphic designer, web designer, CPA, or other professional.
			I keep track of business income/expenses in real time.

			I determined my product best-by dates.
			I purchased home bookkeeping software.
			I identified/embraced new business ideas.
			I made the choice to grow my business – or NOT!

Go to **ReneePottle.com/Profitable-Preserves** to receive a PDF copy of this checklist.

A Plan for Your Business

Basic Information	
Business Name	
Legal Structure/ Entity Type	
Formation Date	
Location/Where Products Prepared	
How Products are Sold/Wholesale/ Retail/Consignment	
Employee Names/Avg. Hours Worked	

Procedures/Responsibilities	
Business Operation Steps/I.E. How is Product Prepared?	
Who is Responsible for Preparing Product?	
Who is Responsible for Shipping Products?	
Who is Responsible for Selling Products?	
Who is Responsible for Product Record Keeping?	
Who is Responsible for Financial Record Keeping?	

Starting Up	
Who is Your Target Market?	
What is Your USP?	
What are Your Initial Products?	
Where are You Selling Your Products?	
How Much Profit Do You Plan to Gain in Year 1?	

Year 2 Projections	
Identify Projected Types and Number of New Products in Year 2	
Identify Projected Profit Numbers for Year 2	
Identify Other Business Changes for Year 2, (new employees, expanded sales outlets, new manufacturing location, etc.).	

Year 3 Projections	
Identify Projected Types and Number of New Products in Year 3	
Identify Projected Profit Numbers for Year 3	
Identify Other Business Changes for Year 3, (new employees, expanded sales outlets, new manufacturing location, etc.)	

Year 4 Projections	
Identify Projected Types and Number of New Products in Year 4	
Identify Projected Profit Numbers for Year 4	
Identify Other Business Changes for Year 4, (new employees, expanded sales outlets, new manufacturing location, etc.)	

Year 5 Projections	
Identify Projected Types and Number of New Products in Year 5	
Identify Projected Profit Numbers for Year 5	
Identify Other Business Changes for Year 5, (new employees, expanded sales outlets, new manufacturing location, etc.)	

Go to **ReneePottle.com/Profitable-Preserves** to receive a PDF copy of this checklist.

Glossary

Articles of Operation/Organization: Document that identifies your new LLC, who its members are, the address, the purpose, etc.

Certified Kitchen: A kitchen licensed by state and/or local food safety authorities. A certified kitchen has been deemed safe for preparing certain food products.

Commercial Kitchen: A commercial kitchen is basically the same thing as a certified kitchen. Commercial kitchens are licensed and deemed safe for food production and storage.

Consignment Sales: Selling to a retail establishment for resale. The seller (you) does not get paid for the items until the reseller (store) actually sells the product to the end consumer.

Co-packer: Also known as a contract packer, a co-packer is a company that makes your product for you to sell, using your recipe. A co-packer may make similar products for several different companies.

Cottage Industry: A business that is operated from your own home instead of from a certified kitchen.

Domain Name: The name that identifies your business on the internet. For example, SeedtoPantry.com or PenandProvisions.com.

FOB: Stands for *freight on board* or *free on board*. It means that the buyer is responsible for the product as soon as it leaves the seller's shipping point.

Food Service Distributor: A company that distributes food to schools, hospitals, restaurants, and other facilities that prepare food for customers.

Made with Organic Ingredients: USDA designation that can be used if your products are made with at least 70% organic ingredients.

Micro business: A small business, usually with fewer than 5 employees and less than $250,000 in annual sales.

MSRP: Stands for *manufacturer's suggested retail price*.

Organic: USDA designation that can be used if your products are made with at least 95-99% organic ingredients. Organic products are grown without synthetic pesticides, GMO stock, hormones, or chemical fertilizers.

Restaurant Supply Store: A store that sells commercial grade cooking equipment, and groceries and paper goods in bulk. A restaurant supply store is a good place to get 25 or 50-pound bags of sugar, plastic hairnets, latex gloves, and heavy-duty cooking pots in one location.

Retail Sales: Selling directly to the end user.

Sales Representative: A sales middle man who represents your products, connecting you with appropriate markets.

Small Business: A business with fewer than 500 employees, and less than $1 million in annual sales.

Soft Spreads: For our purposes, a phrase that collectively describes jam, jelly, fruit butter, conserves, preserves, and marmalade.

Specialty Foods: Foods products made in small quantities, using unique or high-value ingredients.

Target Market: An identified group of people who desire your specific products.

Wholesale Sales: Selling to store or other retail establishments for resale.

Wholesale Bulletin Sample

Your Jam and Jelly Company
Mailing Address
City, State, Zip Code
Telephone Number
Website address
Email address

WHOLESALE BULLETIN – SOFT SPREADS

Applicable Date

UPC #	Item #	Product	Size	Wholesale Price	MSRP
000000000000	Jam 1	Soft Spread example	8 ounces	$3.10/each	$6.20/each
000000000000	Jam 2	Soft Spread example	8 ounces	$3.10/each	$6.20/each
000000000000	Jam 3	Soft Spread example	8 ounces	$3.10/each	$6.20/each
000000000000	Jam 4	Soft Spread example	8 ounces	$3.10/each	$6.20/each

PRODUCT FEATURES

Your product tag line/USP could go here

Case Pack: 12

Product features/benefits (for example)

- "Made from organic ingredients"
- "Made in small batches"
- "We only use ripe, local, berries"

Ordering

- Minimum order – 1/2 case
- Orders shipped within 7 days unless otherwise requested

Terms

- Net 30 days from date of invoice. A finance charge of 1.5% per month will be added to all balances over 30 days.
- Mastercard/Visa accepted
- New accounts please pre-pay or submit credit references

Shipping

- Shipping is FOB *My Location.*
- Items shipped FedEx or least expensive carrier

Resale Certificate

- *My State* retailers must include a copy of their resale certificate or resale tax number with each order.

Business Resources

Bulk Ingredient Suppliers:

- MySpicer (MySpicer.com)
- Oregon Spice (OregonSpice.com)
- The Great American Spice Company (AmericanSpice.com)
- Mizkan America, Inc. (Mizkan.com)

Bookkeeping Software:

- Freshbooks (freshbooks.com)
- Quicken Money Management (Quicken.com)
- QuickBooks (quickbooks.intuit.com)
- Xero (xero.com/us/

Business LLC Templates:

- Northwest Registered Agent (northwestregisteredagent.com)
- eForms (eforms.com)
- Law Depot (lawdepot.com}

Business Naming Aid:

- Dot-o-mater.com

Business Plan Templates:

- U.S. Small Business Association (sba.gov)
- Rocket Lawyer (rocketlawyer.com/form/business-plan.rl#/)
- SCORE (score.org/resource/business-plan-template-startup-business)

Canning Jar Suppliers:

- Uline (Uline.com)
- Berlin Packaging (BerlinPackaging.com)
- Fillmore Container (FillmoreContainer.com)
- Specialty Bottle (SpecialtyBottle.com)
- Bruni Glass (www.bruniglass.com)

Commercial Kitchen Resources:

- Kitchen for Rent (commercialkitchenforrent.com)
- Culinary Incubator (culinaryincubator.com/

Cottage Industry Information:

- Forrager.com
- Homemade for Sale: How to Set Up and Market a Food Business from Home, by Lisa Kivirist and John Ivanko (Book)

Design Software: For business logo, business cards, etc.

- Summitsoft Software (Summitsoft.com). Several affordable options including Logo Design, Graphic Design Studio, Website Creator, Business Card Studio Pro.
- Canva (Canva.com)
- Inkscape Draw Freely (inkscape.org)

Domain Name Check:

- Whois.com

Domain Name Registrar: There are hundreds of domain registrars, and most site hosts also operate as domain registrars. I personally have purchased domains from GoDaddy, Bluehost, and Siteground. The following are currently considered the best registrars – keeping in mind that this may change:

- Domain.com
- GoDaddy.com
- Bluehost.com
- HostGator.com

EIN Number:

- IRS.gov

Food Ingredient Distributors:

- US Foods (USFoods.com)
- Food Services of America (fsafoods.com)
- Sysco (Sysco.com)

Food Innovation Centers:

- North Carolina Food Innovation Lab (ncfoodinnovationlab.org)
- Oregon State University Food Innovation Center (fic.oregonstate.edu/fic/food-product-development)
- Rutgers Food Innovation Center (foodinnovation.rutgers.edu)
- University of Hawaii Maui Food Innovation Center (http://maui.hawaii.edu/foodinnovation/)
- Washington State University Food Processing Extension and Research (foodprocessing.wsu.edu/extension/training/)

Food Preservation Training:

- National Center for Home Food Preservation (nchfp.uga.edu)
- State Cooperative Extension Offices
- Michigan State University (canr.msu.eu)

- USDA Complete Guide to Home Canning 2015(mdc.itap.purdue.edu)
- Simply Canning (online classes, SimplyCanning.com)

Helpful Resources:

- *The Flavor Bible*, by Karen Page and Andy Dornenburg
- *Starting a Part-time Food Business*, by Jennifer Lewis
- *The Magic of Tiny Business*, by Sharon Rowe
- *Sell Your Specialty Food*, by Stephen F. Hall
- *Homemade for Sale: How to Set Up and Market a Food Business from Home*, by Lisa Kivirist and John Ivanko

Label Designers:

- Local Graphic Artists
- Fiverr.com
- Design your own!

Label Making Companies:

- Sticker You (StickerYou.com)
- Labels Plus (LabelsPlus.com)
- Evermine for Business (evermine.com)
- U Printing (UPrinting.com)

Membership Organizations:

- Specialty Food Association (SpecialtyFood.com)

Nutrition Label Testing Labs:

- NutriData (Nutritdata.com)
- Midwest Labs (MidwestLabs.com)
- Food Lab (Foodlab.com)

Online Retail Outlets:

- Etsy (etsy.com)
- Amazon Seller Program (services.amazon.com)

Payment Processing:

- PayPal® (PayPal®.com)
- Google Wallet (Google.com)
- Square (Squareup.com)
- Stripe (Stripe.com)

Restaurant Supply Stores:

- Smart Foodservice Warehouse Stores (Western U.S.)
- Webstaurantstore.com (online)
- FoodServiceDirect.com (online)
- Restaurant Depot (nationwide)
- AllBulkFoods.com (online)

Shipping Companies:

- Fedex® (fedex.com) set up an account for reduced shipping rates
- United Parcel Service/UPS® (ups.com) set up an account for reduced shipping rates
- United States Postal Service® (usps.com)

Small Business Development Centers: Local centers, located all over the U.S., that help you determine how to start and grow your business.

- Sba.gov/

Then click on Local Assistance, then SBA Development Centers, to get information for your State/Municipality

Trademark Electronic Search System:
- Uspto.gov (click Trademark, then Search System)

UPC Label System:
- gs1-us.info

Website Designers:
- Local Graphic Artists
- Fiverr.com
- Design your own!

Website Hosts: This is a business that actually hosts your website. There are various plans, at various price points. Some have a basic point-and-click site building option, while others merely host whatever website you have built from scratch. Some of the best hosts are:
- Siteground.com (currently hosts all my sites)
- Bluehost.com
- HostGator.com
- DreamHost.com

The best website building hosts are considered:
- Wix.com
- Weebly.com
- Squarespace.com

Index

ABOUT THE AUTHOR

Renee Pottle is a writer, author, and serial *side-gig* entrepreneur. She has written several cookbooks, including *Creative Jams and Preserves*, and for many years operated a specialty food company whose products were distributed throughout the Northwest.

Renee's passion for food preservation, and the science behind it, led her to stints as a Master Food Preserver, Nutrition Educator, and a freelance writer specializing in food, food businesses, and small agriculture.

Renee and her husband live in Washington state's sunny Mid-Columbia region, where she grows peaches, raspberries, and way too many tomatoes. In her spare time, she spoils her seven perfect grandchildren, and a one very demanding cat.

Find Renee online at SeedtoPantry.com where she writes about canning/preserving and baking, or at ReneePottle.com for information about her books and other professional writing projects.

Additional Books by Renee Pottle:

Creative Jams and Preserves: Easy Recipes Handcrafted by You

Holiday Gifts from the Kitchen: Cooking with Love

The Confident Canner: Answers to All Your Canning Questions

Homestyle Favorites Made Meatless: Cooking with Meat Substitutes

Spread the Word

If you enjoyed this book and found it helpful, I would be grateful if you would write a review on Amazon, Goodreads, BN.com, your blog, and elsewhere.

Posted reviews help other prospective side-gig entrepreneurs find my books.

I thank you so much, and wish you success on your jam and jelly business journey!

Renee

Printed in Great Britain
by Amazon

31252224R00101